FUTURE FIT

GILES HUTCHINS

AUTHOR OF *THE NATURE OF BUSINESS*
AND *THE ILLUSION OF SEPARATION*

FOREWORD BY

ANTON CHERNIKOV

Design Services: The Write Factor

www.thewritefactor.co.uk

FUTURE FIT

GILES HUTCHINS

'Many books call for new ways of thinking for modern leaders but until *Future Fit* none have provided such wise, well researched and practical approaches to guide leaders facing deeply complex challenges. In this compelling workbook Giles Hutchins is at the forefront of synthesizing new logics for business with the natural rhythms of life and the human mind that will revolutionize business. *Future Fit* is a must-read for every leader who wants to continue being successful or to move beyond what currently feels like impossible challenges. As an experienced Chief Executive I cannot recommend this powerful work highly enough.'
Dr Lynne Sedgmore CBE, Former Chief Executive of 157 Group, Centre for Excellence in Leadership UK, and ranked one of the UK's most influential people in Debretts 2015 List.

'*Future Fit* is a masterpiece of synthesis weaving together the emergent strands of wisdom from others with the author's own extraordinary insights. This is a must-read for any business person seeking answers to a deep inner sense that something different is needed for them and their organization to stay relevant in the 21st century.'
Mark Drewell, Senior Partner, The ForeSight Group, co-founder and former CEO of the Globally Responsible Leadership Initiative

'*Future Fit* is prescient and practical. It describes the future as it can and should be, by drawing on a breadth of knowledge rarely seen in business books. It also makes big, abstract ideas more concrete, by offering examples and advice. This book will help managers navigate a complex world for a more sustainable world. Giles Hutchins is one of the most broad-reaching, forward thinking writers in business.'
Tima Bansal, Canada Research Chair in Business Sustainability, Ivey Business School

*'We see an emerging trend of moving from a mechanistic view of business to an organic, living organization framework, and **Future Fit** goes right to the heart of it. Packed full with practical insights to help activate and catalyze this transformation, this is a brilliant book that will help you wrap your head around the shifting paradigm at the vanguard of future business. Read it!'*
Norman Wolfe, CEO of Quantum Leaders and author of *The Living Organization*

'Hutchins offers lifesaving radical surgery for humanity and the business world. With breath-taking flair, he dismantles illusions and articulates a bold and sophisticated vision of organizational sanity.'
Dr Malcolm Parlett, author of *Future Sense, Five Explorations of Whole Intelligence for a World That's Waking Up.*

*'**Future Fit** is like an encyclopaedia of anecdotes, practical exercises, reflective questions and real life examples set in a very uplifting context to prepare us for the time to come...This book appeals and adds value to all aspects of my life; it will now be my first point of reference for all my personal and professional interventions.'*
Darshita Gillies, Coach, Consultant, Entrepreneur & Co-Founder of Blu Dot

'A treasure-trove of approaches, methods, models and living examples of ways of creating the regenerative organization of the future.'
Peter Hawkins, Professor of Leadership, Henley Business School, author of *Leadership Team Coaching* and many other books

'If you are one of today's leaders who feels the pull toward shaping our emerging future for a better humanity, this book will be your guide.'
Gina Hayden, Co-Founder of the Global Centre for Conscious Leadership

ACKNOWLEDGEMENTS

The explorations, examples, insights and tips in the pages ahead have been inspired by many people, too many to list. Here, I would like to specifically mention some of the people who directly contributed to this book: Anton Chernikov, Peter Hawkins, Malcolm Parlett, Geoff Kendall, Charles Middleton Gina Hayden, Richard Barrett, Sue Carter, James Allen, Dan Burgess, Simon Robinson, Daniel Ludevig, Sue Blagburn, Lorna Howarth and The Write Factor crew; and also the wisdom and love of my wife Star and our two daughters Lilly-Belle and Hazel Grace Hutchins, my dear parents Phil and Diana Hutchins, my sister and her family (The Williams), and my Aunties and Godmothers Daphne Killian, and Merle and Madelaine Hutchins. Thank you!

The title of this book was inspired by conversations over the past two years with Geoff Kendall and Bob Willard of the non-profit Future-Fit Foundation. They define a Future-Fit Business as a company that 'in no way undermines - and ideally increases - the possibility that humans and other life will flourish on Earth forever'. And they're building an open source tool - the Future-Fit Business Benchmark - to help organizations measure how far away they are from reaching that goal. When it comes to non-financial performance, this gives business leaders something they've been sorely lacking: a clear goal to aim for. But to transform toward it, most companies will need to completely rethink the way they do business. And that's where this book comes in: if the Future-Fit Business Benchmark is the 'what', then what you're about to read is the 'how'. To find out more about the Future-Fit Business Benchmark, visit futurefitbusiness.org and for more on this book, visit futurefitbook.com

FOREWORD

In light of our growing economic, social and environmental challenges the only way forward is to make peace with the reality that we must continuously re-invent how we do things. *Future Fit* does nothing more and nothing less than curate the best knowledge from the corners of the world to prepare us all for this new reality of making and re-making; learning and unlearning.

In many ways *Future Fit* is a fusion of Giles's first two books, *The Nature of Business* and *The Illusion of Separation*. It is a practical, and yet also a philosophical, guide for anyone who is involved in for-purpose enterprise. Whether you are starting out as an entrepreneur or are a seasoned business executive, the principles that Giles outlines are timeless and transferrable across all industries, generations and cultures.

This book demonstrates that conscious purpose-driven business, which seeks to distribute value fairly across all stakeholders, is not just some utopian futurist vision, but is something that is happening right now, just as you read this page. It's gone mainstream, and *Future Fit* shows you how to get onboard before you find yourself left behind. As Giles explains, firms of the past find themselves caught up in a top-down, hierarchic, KPI-obsessed, siloed, control-based, and reactive mind-set. Firms of the future are regenerative businesses that operate from a fundamentally different logic. They seek harmony with life: embracing natural ways of being and doing by resonating with the inter-relational, participatory, co-creative nature of living systems innate within our own humanity. Where would you prefer to go to work each day?

Future Fit is a refreshingly pragmatic book that is flooded with practical tips and case studies. Giles has the rare ability to capture the essence of complex systems and address the root causes of any problem. It has been a great privilege to brainstorm and collaborate with Giles over the last year. Together, I hope we can spark more entrepreneurs and business leaders to take a leap of faith and let go of the old business logic, embracing instead a more human, more holistic, more compassionate, more collaborative, more conscious business paradigm.

Finally, if we wish to accelerate toward a more conscious future-fit world we need to apply the principles of this book and share our learning openly. Please visit futurefitbook.com and share with us your views and experiences of this future-fit model. Together, we can leverage the power of future-fit businesses to accelerate us toward a more conscious, collaborative and compassionate world.

– Anton Chernikov, founder of The Exponentials &
IO Collective

CONTENTS

INTRODUCTION

THESE CHALLENGING TIMES ARE
USHERING IN A NEW CONSCIOUSNESS,
RADICALLY ALTERING HOW WE OPERATE
AND ORGANIZE IN BUSINESS
AND BEYOND.

'A DOOR LIKE THIS HAS CRACKED OPEN FIVE OR SIX TIMES SINCE WE GOT UP ON OUR HIND LEGS. IT'S THE BEST POSSIBLE TIME TO BE ALIVE, WHEN ALMOST EVERYTHING YOU THOUGHT YOU KNEW IS WRONG.'

VALENTINE, ARCADIA

EACH GENERATION EXPERIENCES SIGNIFICANT CHANGE due to innovations, disruptions and shifting perspectives transforming our ways of operating and organizing in business and beyond. Yet, the times in which we live herald paradigmic and metamorphic shifts challenging what we do and the way we do it, calling into question our sense of purpose, and demanding wholly new ways of creating and delivering value. This is in part due to the catalytic effect of digitization and globalization, and in part due to the urgent trilemma of economic, environmental and social challenges now upon us. Amid all this, there are complex shifts affecting each of us at deep and partly unconscious levels, challenging how we perceive ourselves, each other and the world around us. At once it is an immensely exciting, liberating, testing and unpredictable time to be involved in the future of business.

This crucial time bears witness to a profound window opening between two worldviews, that of the out-dated yet still prevalent logic of yesterday (with its hallmark models, mind-sets and metrics) and the dawn of our emerging future whereupon the perceptions and practices of yesterday melt amid the heat of the moment, alchemically reconfiguring new pathways, perspectives, principles and behaviors. The ancient Greeks called such a time *Kairos* - a supreme moment of indeterminable time which, if not adequately engaged and acted upon, may pass us by.

'In times of turmoil the danger lies not in the turmoil but in facing it with yesterday's logic.'
Peter Drucker, management specialist

Yesterday's logic is too skewed toward control-based hierarchies, short-termism, domination, competition, separation and the fear-based need for certainty and control. How this logic has come to pervade so much of our personal perceptual horizons, organizational culture and societal consciousness is an essentially philosophical question requiring detailed exploration into the philosophies, mythologies, theologies and socio-economic narratives we have lived through during the history of humanity, so as to understand how these perspectives have influenced our sense of place and purpose within the world, culminating in today's transformative time.

Such a philosophical exploration is not the purpose of this workbook - please refer to my previous book *The Illusion of Separation* (2014) which provides in-depth support for this workbook. What we are concerned with here is how, in business, we can liberate ourselves from this old logic, emancipating our organizations from constructs and conventions that no longer serve us as we embrace our challenging future.

This is a practical workbook for the busy practitioner, leader, change agent, cultural catalyst and social entrepreneur seeking to take an active part in transforming today's business landscape. The reader is taken through a series of modules, each with an executive summary and a number of examples, tips and exploratory questions. In my first book, *The Nature of Business* (2012), a detailed exploration of what constitutes a 'firm of the future' is undertaken and, in particular, how we can apply the regenerative logic of nature's patterns, processes and principles to our own business transformations. Again, this detailed exploration is not what concerns us here, so please refer to *The Nature of Business* as a supporting aid to this workbook where a deeper exploration on this is needed.

There is a detailed Notes section at the end of this book providing signposts to further reading, websites and other support. Every time you come across a [Note] it will refer to further information about what is being conveyed.

Enjoy the ride as we learn to let-go of yesterday's logic while enthusiastically embodying the future of business.

MODULE ONE

A METAMORPHOSIS IN OUR MIDST

FLOURISHING FUTURE-FIT BUSINESS REQUIRES US TO GO BEYOND THE SURFACE AND SYMPTOMATIC INTO TRANSFORMING MIND-SETS AT DEEP AND PARTLY UNCONSCIOUS LEVELS.

EXECUTIVE SUMMARY

- Increasing volatility, complexity and uncertainty is the new norm, hence our organizations need to be able to not just survive but thrive amidst unceasing transformation.

- Too many of today's organizations are locked in to a logic that is strangling their ability to adapt and evolve amid volatility.

- Isolated initiatives such as wellbeing-at-work, purposeful business, and corporate responsibility, often leave the underlying logic, culture and ethos of the organization unchecked.

- Only a fundamental overhaul of the underlying logic will enable our firms of the future to flourish amid these transformational times.

'WHAT THE CATERPILLAR CALLS THE END
OF THE WORLD, THE MASTER CALLS
THE BUTTERFLY.'
RICHARD BACH, AUTHOR

SINCE THE INDUSTRIAL REVOLUTION, WE have achieved great
feats of economic, social and technological advancement. The
structures and strictures of old have served us well in many material
ways. But, as Bob Dylan would say, 'times they are a changing!'

We now face increasing volatility on numerous fronts: enter the
world of commodity spikes, resource scarcity, widespread
environmental degradation, social inequality, economic
turbulence, population and migrant pressure, changing
demographics, the internet of things, disruptive technologies,
climate change, and more.

Over half the world's population is now younger than 30 years
old. Two generations have now grown up with the internet. It
doesn't take a degree in anthropology to notice that the world is
very different today than it was 30 years ago. [Note 1]

In 2010, 1.2 billion people were online globally. By 2020, that
number will reach 5 billion. Nearly 4 billion more people, along
with their collective intelligence, will be available for value
creation via smartphones, tablets and internet cafés. The
capabilities being unleashed are unprecedented.

Uber, the world's largest taxi company, owns no vehicles;
Facebook, the world's most popular media owner, creates no
content; Alibaba, the most valuable retailer, has no inventory;
Airbnb, the world's largest accommodation-provider, owns no
real estate. The institutional and ownership powers of old are
being challenged by the empowering effect of the network.

The best people do not want to work in bureaucratic
organizations. They want to be in an environment that is
creative, exciting, empowering, purposeful and passionate. They
want to feel a meaningful connection with the value they create,

rather than feeling like lost corporate cogs enslaved in the monolith of machine mentality.

What many of us crave for are more meaningful moments and life-experiences. More time to spend following our curiosity; to feel alive and explore our authenticity. More time to build nourishing relationships; to really experience the world as well as what is around us here and now. More time to enjoy the simple things in life; to be present with our loved ones, with our friends, acquaintances and strangers we meet along the way. Yet much of the time our working life starves us of what is most precious to us, the time and space to become who we truly are: social, curious, playful, creative, loving and purposeful humans.

We all know that at one level our current business paradigm has created immense material wealth yet has also exacerbated the imbalances, tensions and volatility we face today. We also know that the business models and management approaches that served us well in the past are no longer fit for this fast-changing future. Business-as-usual is no longer an option.

Conferences, think-tanks, research papers, workshops, forums and expert roundtables across the globe are exploring the implications these challenges have on how we operate and organize. Yet, through our well-intended desire to find solutions, we all-too-often find ourselves caught up in the very mind-set that contributed to our problems in the first place. We address our sea of challenges at face-value and in largely siloed and reductive ways, skimming over the deeper inter-relational corruptions these problems are symptomatic of.

Whether it's the shift to more purposeful business, dealing with climate change, embracing the digitized Millennial Age, CSR, wellbeing-at-work, diversity in the workplace, the future world-of-working, employee empowerment, stakeholder engagement, etc., what underpins and interweaves all these initiatives is a deeper underlying metamorphosis of epic proportions. Caught up as we are in our stressful schedules, we struggle to see the forest from the trees, perceiving these initiatives as disparate topics vying for our attention. Yet, the more conscious we are of the tectonic shifts these surface waves are symptomatic of, the more able we are to help our organizations become future-fit.

Put simply, the most important challenge and opportunity facing our leaders, managers, and change agents today is our ability to embrace a deep and fundamental shift in logic - a shift in how we think, perceive and relate - amid the busyness of today's frenetic work-life.

Let's stand back for a brief moment in order to gain perspective on how acculturated and habituated we have become – individually and collectively - by a dominant mode of thinking-and-doing which is not just undermining the effectiveness of our organizations, it is actually undermining our humanity, and the very fabric of life on Earth. As one of America's most admired CEO's, Ray Anderson, succinctly put it, 'we have been, and still are, in the grips of a flawed view of reality – a flawed paradigm, a flawed worldview – and it pervades our culture putting us on a biological collision course with collapse' (Note 2) We now know beyond question that our dominant way of living and working is severely corrupting the fabric of life, leading to all sorts of unravelling ramifications for the kind of future we leave our children, undermining the evolutionary potential not just of our human species but of all our other fellow kinship on this Earth. As entrepreneur, author, and founder of the Natural Capital Institute, Paul Hawken, aptly notes, 'At present, we are stealing the future, selling it in the present, and calling it GDP.' (Note 3)

But to really challenge this tyranny of reductive short-termism undermining our humanity, we need to deal with underlying causes.

So let's cut to the chase. The root cause of our carcinogenic corporate mind-set is a corrupting logic that sets us apart from, and in competition with, our own true nature, each other and the world around us. We have become inured in a flawed philosophic and socio-economic worldview which pervades our daily consciousness to such an extent that much of our collective activity assumes it to be just-the-way-life-is.

What we consider normal business practice is often pathological. We struggle to see beyond this pathology, caught up in our own illusory hall of mirrors creating what Albert Einstein called an optical delusion of consciousness. We are engaged in a kind of deluding neurosis with devastating implications for human society and the wider fabric of life on Earth. And, our ingrained approaches to education, economics and organizational management are, in the main, infected by this neurosis, exacerbating the acculturation of our insanity.

Time is not on our side. If we wish to ensure anything resembling a successful outcome for our organizations, wider socio-economic systems and general civilization, we need to get radical and deal with root causes while also attending to downstream effects.

Such a shift challenges us at deep and partly unconscious levels. It challenges powerful and complex influences within our own psyche and cultural consciousness. It challenges the status quo structures of governance, engrained patterns of power relations, and dominant ways of leading, managing and operating within our organizations. It challenges the very way in which we relate as human beings in our more-than-human world.

Sounds daunting - yet there is good news: this fundamental and profound metamorphosis is nothing more, nor nothing less, than an opening up to who we naturally are. In the pages ahead what we explore is emancipation from what has become an enslaving logic. And with this emancipating shift in logic, we can experience what it really means to be fully human in a firm of the future.

> 'Emancipate yourselves from mental slavery, none but ourselves can free our minds.'
> *Bob Marley, musician*

The metaphor of a metamorphosis is a powerful one for the times we are in, and we like the beautiful metamorphosis of the caterpillar to the butterfly for obvious reasons. In the early stages of the caterpillar's metamorphosis to a butterfly, the caterpillar undergoes a 'breakdown' phase where the structures of old begin to dissolve. Amid this breakdown, 'imaginal cells' start to form clusters called 'imaginal groupings'. These imaginal cells are always present within the caterpillar (always present within our human systems) yet it is only amid the conditions of breakdown that they form these groupings. The caterpillar, still inured in the logic of yesterday, uses vital energy (antibodies and such like) to fight these groupings, sensing them as a threat to the status quo. With time, and the persistence of these imaginal groupings, a tipping point or threshold starts to be crossed within the caterpillar (and within the consciousness of our own organizational systems). The imaginal groupings are seen for what they are, prototyping the future, and with that vital energy is used to nourish them rather than undermine them, and quite quickly the metamorphic process unfolds.

We are living in a time of thresholds being crossed, and the more conscious we are of these shifts the more able we are to help metamorphose our dominant logic.

CROSSING THE THRESHOLD

Mechanistic	⇨	Living
Linear	⇨	Inter-relational
Extractive	⇨	Regenerative
Dominator	⇨	Partner
Power over	⇨	Power with
Trade-offs	⇨	Synergies
Dog-eat-dog competition	⇨	Collaboration across boundaries
Short-termism	⇨	Inter-generational
Exclusive	⇨	Inclusive
Ego	⇨	Soul
Anthropocentric	⇨	More-than-human world

By characterizing this shift in logic as going from one general set of characteristics to another, we risk over-simplifying something emergent and complex into something linear and binary; in-so-doing we are at risk of applying the very logic we are attempting to transcend into our map of the way beyond it.

On the other hand, it is useful for our conceptualizing, analyzing, thinking minds to have this shift defined in such a way. It is helpful for us to grasp on to something, and so shifts from 'old to new' will be used here with this caveat in mind: this is a shift into a way of attending that is inclusive of all ways of perceiving (including the mind-set of old which has its useful place within a holistic array of perceptions). We are not throwing the baby-out-with-the-bath-water here. Yesterday's logic, with its narrowing-down constricting perspective, brings something useful into our horizon of awareness. The problem comes when this perspective dominates. Then, we fail to fully perceive the inter-relationality of our world. We become blinkered to the interdependencies and synergies, blinding ourselves to the exploitative impacts of our actions. Enter Einstein's optical delusion of consciousness. It is this that we are transcending.

REFLECTIVE QUESTIONS

How comfortable are you about the fact that our prevalent way of living - which is fast being exported to all corners of our global human community – is destroying some of the things we cherish most?

What kind of future do you think we are currently leaving for our children and grand-children?

Do you believe that you and your organization could become a force for good in the world, creating conditions that enhance rather than degrade life?

What initiatives can you think of in your organization, sector, or stakeholder community that seek to move toward a brighter future?

Which of these initiatives are incremental to the current business mind-set of short-term profit maximization, and which are innovations beyond it?

Try and recall or imagine what the world was like 30 years ago, before mobile phones, remote working, the internet and Facebook. Now cast your mind forward to 30 years hence and envision what you would like the world to be like?

What kind of working environment would you like to be working in, in say five years' time, and what sort of organization do you dream your children could work in when they are old enough?

MODULE **TWO**

FIRM OF THE FUTURE

OUR 20TH CENTURY MECHANISTIC
MIND-SET IS OUTDATED, FIT ONLY FOR
FIRMS OF THE PAST. OUR FIRMS OF THE
FUTURE APPLY LIVING-SYSTEMS LOGIC
TO THRIVE IN THE VOLATILE
TIMES AHEAD.

EXECUTIVE SUMMARY

- These are exciting yet challenging times for the future of business. We need to simultaneously liberate ourselves from old ways of working and embrace new methods and practices, while keeping the wheels on the road rolling.

- This new business logic is essentially about becoming 'regenerative'.

- Regenerative business shifts our frame of thinking from a linear, reductive and siloed perspective to relational multi-stakeholder systems-thinking that seeks collaboration, shared value and co-production.

- Firms of the future prioritize relationships and nurture a spirit of community based on shared values and synergy.

- The over-arching vision of a firm of the future is to be in service of life, to create value for ourselves while leaving the place richer for future generations; it is simply good business sense.

'ANY COMPANY DESIGNED FOR SUCCESS IN THE 20TH CENTURY IS DOOMED TO FAILURE IN THE 21ST CENTURY.'

DAVID S. ROSE, SERIAL ENTREPRENEUR

THERE IS AN OLD CHINESE proverb that says, 'In times of great winds, some build bunkers, others build windmills.' We are living in these times of great winds. Winds of change are blowing through us challenging each and every organization. The now trendy managerial acronym VUCA (volatile, uncertain, complex and ambiguous) goes a long way in describing this business context we find ourselves in. We are not just dealing with transformation; we are dealing with unceasing transformation. Such times of uncertainty and volatility naturally invoke fear in us, yet it is a fearful clinging to the tried-and-tested status quo that will undermine our ability to adapt and evolve in these challenging times.

It is now quite apparent that many of our organizations and leaders are ill-equipped to deal with the situation ahead of us. For instance, the global business service provider IBM undertook an extensive survey of more than 1,500 CEOs from 60 countries and 33 industries worldwide and found that there is a significant 'complexity gap' in our leaders' ability to deal with the volatile times ahead. This is a systemic problem with its roots in yesterday's logic. Too many of today's organizations find themselves caught up in a top-down, hierarchic, KPI-obsessed, siloed, control-based, defensive and reactive fire-fighting mind-set. It is this that undermines and erodes the greatness of our workplaces, turning them into places of drudgery, stress, political infighting and ineffective bureaucracies. This monocultural mechanistic mentality stifles the natural creativity, innovation, collaboration, reciprocity, conviviality and empathy we humans exude when allowed to be our natural selves. So often, we find ourselves bound to artificial constructs and interventions that seek to control and manage us, yet actually undermine our vitality and wellbeing and so end up undermining the viability and resilience of the organization. As organizational specialist John Seddon notes:

'command-and-control management has created service organizations that are full of waste, offer poor service, depress the morale of those who work in them and are beset with management functions that not only do not contribute to improving the work, but actually make it worse. The management principles that have guided the development of these organizations are logical – but it's the wrong logic.' (Note 1)

Attempting to transform our ways of operating and organizing toward more human, resilient and flourishing businesses without addressing this flawed mind-set is like applying the preverbal Band-Aid to a systemic illness. In the words of Dawn Vance, Nike's Director of Global Logistics:

> 'Organizations have 3 options:
>
> Hit the wall;
>
> Optimise and delay hitting the wall; or
>
> Redesign for resilience' (Note 2)

The word 'resilience' here does not just mean the ability to 'withstand' change, as change upon change is what characterizes our future and we need to do far more than withstand, we need to adapt, flex and thrive in our transforming landscape. This is what Nassim Taleb means by his phrase 'anti-fragile' in his book of the same title. Anti-fragile organizations thrive in uncertainty. As Taleb notes, the tragedy of the top-down control-based logic inherent in so many of today's organizations is that it deprives us of sensing and responding to change, it numbs us from dealing with uncertainty and so it fails us. In reality, our search for control closes us off from real life. (Note 3)

Another important aspect of what we mean by resilience here is longevity. By longevity we mean the ability to thrive over the long-term rather than mere short-term growth bubbles soon ending in collapse.

The extractive, short-termist, self-maximizing, control-based, ego-orientated logic haunting so many of today's organizations has a history. Born out of a militarized mind and honed through the Industrial Age, bureaucracies emerged through economies of scale. Centralized management and control removed decision-making from the undertaking of work itself as hierarchies of managers became separated from workers. Along came the scientific management thinking of Taylorism, industrial and post-industrial productization, and the quantification-obsessed ethos of management-by-numbers. Add to this: the cultural norms of a patriarchal dominator logic (the accumulation of power through control over others); modern Western scientific-philosophy dominated by rationalism (a reductive atomizing, categorizing and organizing of the world into neatly definable objectified chunks); a scientific logic of anthropocentric materialism (the world around us is objectified and desacralized into 'resources' to be exploited for human betterment); a socio-economic logic heavily influenced by Social Darwinism (human self-agency is understood as innately selfish, life is seen as nothing more than a struggle for survival, and evolution a process of selfish ascendency where we either dominate or become dominated in a dog-eat-dog world). It is no small wonder we have ended up with the paradigm we have. (Note 4)

'The whole philosophy of Hell rests on a recognition of the axiom that...'To be' means 'to be in competition'.
C. S. Lewis, academic and novelist (Note 5)

Enter the now urgent need to reinvent, reorganize and reconfigure our ways of creating and delivering value. In our hearts-and-souls we know that our work can be meaningful, creating value for ourselves, each other and the more-than-human world we form a part of.

REGENERATIVE BUSINESS

The word 'regenerative' means creating the conditions conducive for life to continuously renew itself and flourish. The primary principle underpinning our firms of the future is 'regenerative', where organizations help rather than hinder the evolutionary dynamic of life. This goes beyond traditional CSR initiatives as it is not primarily aimed at reducing negative impacts or 'externalities' created by the current mind-set; rather, it is a move to an entirely new mind-set, a 'new way' of being and doing in business and beyond.

With this regenerative logic: externalities become opportunities for additional value creation; waste of one output becomes food for another; stakeholders become partners to engage with through authentic communications and reciprocating relations; linear-thinking is replaced with systems-thinking and circular economics; resources are not simply managed and controlled for short-term gain but perceived holistically in the wider context of the inter-relational matrix of life. We re-train ourselves to think 'out-of-the-box', transcending the rigid framing of yesterday's logic, in fact 'the box' is no longer there at all, being replaced with interconnecting patterns of relations, where differing stakeholder perspectives and shifting contexts are appreciated for the diverse perspectives they provide while prototyping richer ways of creating and delivering value.

The metaphor of the machine served us well in the Industrial Age; the metaphor of the living system serves us well in the early 21st Century.

Living systems thrive through relationships. We can allow the boundaries of our silos within and between our organizations to permeate more readily upon realizing that the life-blood of our agility, creativity and resilience flows through our relations. Whereas machine-mentality encourages a hardening of boundaries in order to atomize, control, protect and maximize (leading to siloed mentality, group-think, them-and-us separations, etc.) regenerative systems-thinking encourages a permeating of boundaries for collaboration, shared value and co-innovation (while still respecting security, safety, local customs, and differing cultural values and ownership approaches).

The slogan of old was 'it's all about the numbers', or 'it's all about the economy'. This school of thought is now giving way to a deeper recognition that its actually 'all about relationships', social, environmental and economic relations which create holistic value for life, where business creates healthy and vibrant solutions for ourselves, our future generations and wider more-than-human kinship, as opposed to selling the future for the benefit of the select few in the present.

> 'Ultimately, we want to leave the world a little better than we found it.'
> *Mike Putman, Business Unit President, Skanska UK*

A mainstream business culture which profits at the expense of society and our environment will only lead us toward a destructive 'Easter Island' scenario. It creates what Alain De Botton refers to as Status Anxiety; which is what Western (and

emerging economies) are increasingly infected with today. (Note 7)
Rather than the economy generating wellbeing for the majority
it provides wealth for a minority and anxiety for the majority.
This is not what business needs to be about. Good business is
that of entrepreneurs and business people across the globe
applying their acumen to solving business challenges through
ingenuity and dedication in order to generate value for ourselves,
each other and our more-than-human home. Talented, well-
rounded, values-led individuals are turned-on by business and its
value-creation potential, motivated to contribute their unique
sparks to the economic engine for the benefit of themselves and
the wider whole. (Note 8)

> 'The organization of the future will be an embodiment of
> community based on shared purpose calling on the higher
> aspirations of people.'
> *Dee Hock, founder of VISA*

EXAMPLE: The values that guide Johnson & Johnson are known
as 'Our Credo' and firmly put the needs and well-being of the
people the organization serves first. Robert Wood Johnson,
former chairman from 1932 to 1963 and a member of the
Company's founding family, crafted Our Credo himself in 1943,
just before Johnson & Johnson became a publicly traded
company. This was long before anyone ever heard the term
'corporate social responsibility'. Our Credo is more than just a
moral compass for Johnson & Johnson it's a recipe for business
success. The fact that Johnson & Johnson is one of only a
handful of companies that have flourished through more than a
century of change is proof of that.

>―

Regenerative business goes beyond new leadership techniques, sustainable product innovation, process re-engineering, and the crafting of purposeful mission statements and ethical values charters. Regenerative business is a fundamentally different logic, a timeless logic, drawing on the deep wisdom of life.

While we know it will be radically different from the firm of the past, we cannot define what the firm of the future will become in neat objectified ways as, by its very nature, it is metamorphic, emergent and adaptive, organically shape-shifting with the changing business context.

It is in our nature to wish to seek clarity and definition in the midst of an ever-changing future, and this is in part what fuels our desire to make-sense of what is emerging. The pages ahead offer insights, examples and qualities of what a firm of the future looks and feels like, but this is not a 'cook-book' offering a prescriptive methodology, rather it is an exploration into unchartered waters. We may take reassurance and inspiration from others in their explorations yet each of our organizations will embark on our own journeys toward becoming a firm of the future in myriad ways, some choosing to hold on to more of yesterday's logic than others who choose to embrace more radical transfigurations.

The good news is that business can take inspiration from living systems all around us. Many organizations have been doing this successfully for some time already through various approaches such as biomimetic product design, biophilic workplaces, closed-loop economics, industrial ecology, wild leadership quests, deep nature immersions, and so forth. Yet regenerative business goes beyond a superficial mimicking of living systems or temporary escapades through nature quests, as it seeks an entire reframing of the business model within regenerative 'living' logic, embedded at all levels of organizing and operating.

This 'new way' seeks harmony with life: embracing natural ways of being and doing by resonating with the inter-relational, participatory, co-creative nature of living systems innate within our own humanity and throughout our more-than-human world. As the ancient Stoic philosopher Seneca noted, 'True wisdom consists in not departing from Nature and in molding our conduct according to Her laws and model'. The over-arching vision of a firm of the future is to work with the grain of nature, creating value for ourselves while leaving the place richer for future generations.

> 'Regeneration is the ethical imperative of our age.
> We cannot settle for half measures.'
> *Gregory Landua, CEO of Terra Genesis International* (Note 8)

Regenerative-thinking goes beyond the preservation and restoration of our human communities and natural ecosystems. It is about operating in ways that contribute, replenish and evolve within the evolution of life: business that is not just copying living systems logic but deeply embodying this logic, finding harmony within the rhythms, flows and evolutionary currents of the natural systems we call 'Life'. It provokes a whole raft of practical challenges and opportunities for our innovative minds to create value-based solutions for, and it also provokes a deep philosophical yet no less practical inquiry into who we truly are, what our deeper sense of purpose is, and to whom our organizations seek to serve?

In short, a firm of the future serves Life; in-so-doing it enriches ourselves and our customers and wider stakeholder ecosystem. To materially benefit our customers while damaging the fabric of life for others is a hallmark of the firm of the past and its old logic; such short-termism is no longer a viable business proposition for the firm of the future.

'The closer we dance to the rhythms and patterns that lie
within us, the closer we get to acting in what is the
right way.'
HRH The Prince of Wales

This is a radical change in our perception of business and our
work ethic: from it being a means to an end, a vehicle for paying
the bills and acquiring power, control and material wealth; to
dedicating our time, resources and creativity to initiatives that
serve Life. This transforms our role and purpose from an
essentially acquisitive 'what's-in-it-for-me' approach toward a
mind-set of compassion and contribution, which brings vitality
and wellbeing to all our living systems; for ourselves, our local
neighbors, our global citizens, our children and our more-than-
human kinship. In-so-doing, we wake up to what it really means
to be fully human.

EXAMPLE: A professional academy institution in Canada, The
International Academy of Collaborative Professionals, working
with lawyers and other professions has started to explore the
benefits of embedding a time-honored practice into its core
decision making process. Likewise, organizations affiliated with
the institution have started to bring this simple yet powerful
practice into their decision-making process to great effect. This
practice is referred to by Mac Macartney of Embercombe as the
'children's fire'. It is an ancient indigenous practice of placing the
livelihood of our children at the heart of our decision-making,
so that every time an important strategic or operational decision
is undertaken, we consider the impact it will have on the
livelihood of our children (for indigenous cultures it is the next
seven generations of children, but just looking to the next
generation is a good first step for our short-termist lens to start
adjusting to). It begs the question: what kind of organization is it
that doesn't value the livelihood of our children?

At first glance, this requirement to understand and consider the impact on the next generation of our business decisions can seem like an additional burden that we could well do without in the midst of challenging and competitive climes. Yet what those embracing this practice have come to experience is that, far from it being a burden, it is a blessing as it opens up vistas of perception at the heart of our decision making process, resulting in far richer, resilient and wiser routes being taken.

>~~~

So what does regenerative business look and feel like in practice?

There is a general shift away from narrowly controlling the silos of business functions into a widening of our perceptual horizon to perceive the relations across our organization and across our business ecosystem of stakeholders. Each of us takes personal responsibility for understanding the dynamics of relations in our sphere of influence, and seeks to enhance the synergistic value-creation potential of these relationships, not in a 'trade-off' win-win or win-lose kind of way, but in a deeper more human - more natural, heartfelt and authentic - way of creating and delivering value for Life. This involves us really listening and sharing with others to creatively explore and empathically understand the tensions of challenges and opportunities in our sphere of influence.

While being focused on our area of responsibility, we are also continually scanning our emerging landscape and learning to 'read' the emerging future, sensing and responding to new information, opportunities and challenges that arise. We work in self-organizing, locally-attuning ways continually prototyping, presencing and future-scenario planning as we go. This is a far-cry from the top-down machine mentality of much of today's corporations, but it is an essential shift if our firms are to flourish in the years ahead.

Hence, of great importance for embedding this regenerative logic into our organizations, is each of us learning to cultivate our deeper, fuller humanity through the coherence of our natural ways of knowing: intuiting, sensing, and perceiving, as well as cognitively analyzing, the flows, feelings, exchanges and moods of all relations as they emerge and evolve in our ever-changing landscapes. We each must take personal responsibility for developing our capacity for empathy, reciprocity, receptivity and responsiveness, learning to embed these qualities into the collective intelligence of our teams.

There is a shift from problem solving, fire-fighting and fixing conflicts to a wider recognition amongst all stakeholders that we are all responsible for and involved in the emergent future field of possibility. Disagreements, challenges, limitations and misunderstandings act as crucibles for deeper exploration, yet there is less of a struggle over the current situation and more of a striving toward improving our collective co-evolving future through generative conversations, feedback and intimate on-going dialogue between stakeholders. Divergence between different stakeholder groups and individuals is healthy, as it is this diversity that creates differing viewpoints which deepens what emerges. The challenge is how to allow for convergence within this divergence through integration and harmonization across different teams, disciplines, regions and stakeholder communities. Key stakeholders become partners who share responsibility for how we are all sensing and responding to the emerging future, ever conscious of our participatory dynamism.

Old mind-sets die hard and the biggest barrier to progress will be yesterday's logic creeping in at every turn. The quicker areas of misunderstanding and mismatched expectations are revealed the better. We are all in this together, and the more effective we are at co-creating in constructive ways, the more successful we shall be.

Our day-to-day responsibility is to remind ourselves and others to be as true to our authentic selves, our deeper sense of purpose and our organizations' sense of purpose (which is ultimately to enrich our humanity and the wider fabric of life). The richness of our reciprocity determines the quality of value shared and delivered for the partners involved. The more we attune with the ever-changing landscape, the more we sense subtly lit pathways of synchronicity and potential dead-ends, helping us navigate these volatile unchartered waters with our soul-compass.

The entire undertaking of work becomes regenerative, and so our work helps enhance our experience of life in general, and vice versa: continuously learning to let-go, embracing the new, failing and trying again; learning to be patient, empathize, listen, sense, let-go, open-up, move-forward. The 'quest' or 'mission' of this regenerative business is our human drive toward being more alive, more present, more creative, more authentic, more in-the-flow.

FIRM OF THE PAST		FIRM OF THE FUTURE
Top-down hierarchy	⇨	Locally-attuned
Controlling ethos	⇨	Learning ethos
Remote management by numbers	⇨	Distributed decision-making
Bureaucratic	⇨	Participatory
Exploitative	⇨	Empowering
Shareholder focus	⇨	Multi-stakeholder perspective
Monocultural homogenization	⇨	Diversity within community
For-profit	⇨	For-purpose

In *The Nature of Business* a set of Business Principles for firms of the future is explored in detail based on work undertaken by Biomimicry for Creative Innovation (BCI). [Note 9] Here we refer to these Business Principles as 'ways of doing', as they influence how we go about doing things in our organizations, and are complimented by 'ways of being' explored later. [Note 10]

These ways of doing (when infused with the 'ways of being' explored in Module Five) create the regenerative business conditions conducive for life: collaboration, adaptability, creativity, local attunement, multi-functionality and responsiveness; hence, enhancing the evolution of organizations from rigid, tightly managed hierarchies to dynamic living organizations which thrive within ever-changing socio-economic and environmental conditions. Organizations that understand how to embed these principles into their workplaces, products, processes, policies and practices create greater abundance for themselves and their business ecosystems in times of rapid change; flourishing rather than perishing in volatile business conditions.

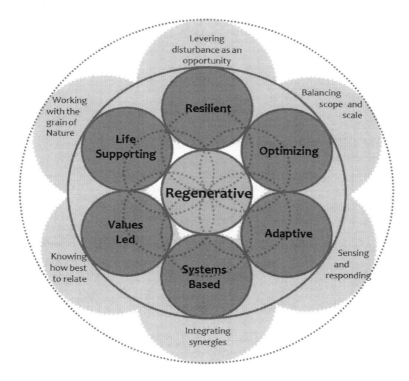

Detailed studies have been undertaken by the Global LAMP Index over ten year periods, comparing the financial performance of organizations embracing living systems principles with their mechanistic counterparts, consistently showing that these living systems principles make for better financial returns and longer term financial resilience. Joseph

Bragdon from the Global LAMP Index notes, 'As an investment manager I have discovered that the more companies model themselves on living systems (as distinct from mechanistic systems) and the deeper they go into aligning themselves with life, the more creative and profitable they become.' (Note 11)

Firms of the future are resilient, optimizing, adaptive, systems-based, values-led, and life-supporting; let's touch on each of these 'ways of doing' briefly here (for more on this see *The Nature of Business*).

RESILIENCE

As mentioned already, resilience is the ability not to just withstand unpredictable shocks but also to thrive in uncertainty, to leverage disturbance as opportunity. The more resilient an organization is, the more able it is to rapidly flex and evolve. Hence, resilience is fast becoming the 'holy grail' for businesses in these increasingly volatile times. Three important attributes for fostering resilience in our organizations are: decentralization, distribution and diversity. The more diverse, decentralized and distributed the business and its network is, the more able it is to seek out opportunities and capitalize upon a changing business landscape.

> 'Decentralization, combined with empowerment, fosters innovation. Through collaboration, these innovations are shared, improved upon, and diffused, multiplying their effect.'
> *Raj Sisodia, co-founder of Conscious Capitalism*

EXAMPLE: Adnams, a UK Brewery, was able to leverage the shock of the 2009 economic crisis as an opportunity. It sensed and responded, rather than dwelled, and utilized the opportunity to reassess the way in which its business works during a cultural and attitudinal shift. Investing in more diversity in its business model approach allowed it to move into adjacent markets, such as spirits, while evolving from dealing 25% of volume with two big customers toward an ecosystem of smaller customers, providing significant increased resilience amid difficult market conditions. Staff empowerment and stakeholder engagement initiatives encouraged people to take local decisions more effectively, leading to more distributed decision-making. While the core market declined due to the economic climate and the switch from on to off-trade, a more diverse product and client portfolio led to short term improvements while embedding strategic resilience into the business, resulting in Adnams outperforming the market in terms of beer volumes sold. (Note 12)

OPTIMIZING

Maximization is driven through homogenizing, scaling up, atomizing, industrializing and reducing complexities within a specific business function, system or process; optimization is driven through enhanced connections, interactivity and interdependencies across different business functions, systems or processes. Maximization brings benefit of economies of scale through lower unit cost of production, hence it has become the hallmark of our monocultural mind-set driving out efficiencies through homogenization, yet what is often overlooked is that it also comes at the expense of economies of scope (synergies gained through diverse connections and interactivity). It is about finding the right sweet spot of scale versus scope for the area of business and stage of maturity (or phase of 'adaptive cycle' – explained shortly) within different parts of the organization.

EXAMPLE: Just prior to the economic crisis Adnams re-organized into more separate, siloed, business units. At a time when rapid change and collaboration was needed to deal with the unfolding global crisis, it quickly sensed the reduction in synergies brought about through the separation of business functions and the reduced collaboration between parts of the business. Sensing and responding to this quickly, it returned to a more integrated functional approach, where economies of scope were realized more readily through better interconnections and enhanced empowerment.

***

'Change in nature happens everywhere, all the time, in a self-organizing urge that comes from every cell and every organism, with no need for central command and control to get orders or pull levels.'
Frederic Laloux, organizational specialist (Note 13)

In nature, the ability for organisms to co-operate, optimize and synergize within their environment is fundamental for their successful evolution. Life is not simply a competitive struggle, more it's an interwoven interplay of co-operative partnerships; the more reciprocating inter-relations the ecosystem supports, the more able it is to deal with volatility; ditto for the living systems of our own organizations.

ADAPTIVE

In the words of Charles Darwin, 'It is not the strongest species that survive, nor the most intelligent, but the ones most able to adapt to change'. Our organizations' ability to adapt relies heavily on the local attunement of teams, quickly and effectively sensing and responding to changing local conditions. Hierarchies of bureaucracy and control along with rigid silos impede organizational adaptability. What our firms of the future need is more collaboration, more connection, and more shared innovation across different departments and business units, and also across diverse partners within the business ecosystem. With the application of social media and collaboration tools, multi-disciplinary teams of people from different organizations can quickly form together, collaborate and prototype solutions and then test them out in the market place without too much upfront investment.

By example, a social enterprise called The Exponentials applies a Brainstorm, Sprint, Share methodology to do just this, bringing diverse stakeholders together to dive deep into a problem and ideate potential solutions. The organizer of the brainstorm then writes everything up into a concise presentation that can be shared to spark a new brainstorm. In some cases a prototype is made (e.g. a clickable app or website using free digital tools like Wix.com, InvisionApp.com and Typeform). These investment-light fast turn-around cycles mean we are always validating our learning while engaging diverse stakeholders through the innovation journey.

Co-innovation partnerships (two or more organizations openly collaborating on a range of activities) and open innovation approaches (where organizational boundaries become far more permeable, with ideas openly exchanged, and collaborative prototyping activities embracing a range of interested parties including the general public) along with co-creation hubs, open innovation platforms and face-to-face gatherings, are all becoming the 'new norm', challenging the ownership and control mechanisms of our old ways. (Note 14)

EXAMPLE: Whole Foods, a large chain of organic health food stores throughout North America, has a light-weight central function that handles certain purchasing, infrastructure and administration functions for the whole group, with each of its stores empowered to take decisions locally. When one store decided to try out installing a bar selling alcoholic and non-alcoholic beverages to customers within its store, it did so without needing to gain central buy-in and approval. Much to the dismay of many on-lookers, it became a huge success. Soon, other Whole Foods stores got in touch and started to share ideas across the company intranet about what could work for their respective stores. There wasn't inter-store rivalry (like is often found between the business unit silos of corporations) only a spirit of sharing so that everyone could work out what was best for their area while collaborating with others. Some stores found it worked well for them, others went for cafés, and some went for neither, all of them sensing and responding to local needs within a global framework which encouraged, rather than stifled, local collaboration and innovation. (Note 15)

EXAMPLE: Virgin has created more than 400 branded companies worldwide, employing approximately 60,000 people in 30 countries. The company operates as a structure of loosely linked autonomous units run by self-managed teams that share a brand name and values. There is no central HQ nor are financials consolidated for a group view. The only central function is Virgin Management Ltd which provides advisory services to all companies within the group and also has specialist sector and regional teams. 'Our companies are part of a family rather than a hierarchy. They are empowered to run their own affairs, yet the companies help one another, and solutions to problems often come from within the Group somewhere. In a sense we are a commonwealth, with shared ideas, values, interests and goals.' (Note 16)

SYSTEMS-BASED

Organizations, like all living systems, are lit up by interconnections and networks of relationships that find success by being both systems-focused and self-focused. We develop this systems perspective by seeing beyond silos into the relations that permeate our boundaries across our organizations and wider business ecosystem.

People are empowered by being connected to a vibrant network of relations, where the success of the community depends on the success of each member and vice versa. Empowerment of individuals empowers the network; likewise empowerment of the community empowers the individuals. For instance, the Japanese mobile industry and its iMode ecosystem, Apple's iTunes/iOS and Google's Android platform as ecosystems all thrive through principles of mutuality within content and service provision. Control mechanisms and bureaucracy simply get in the way of open, emergent, reciprocating networks of diverse inter-relations. Whether it be Facebook or crowd-funding, co-innovation or creative commons, these systems thrive by encouraging connectivity and community; hence transforming the old lenses (power, competition and control) into new eyes (empowering, collaborating and connecting).

'The vast changes required for creating a regenerative society will not be achieved just by reacting to crises after crises. They will require inspiration, aspiration, imagination, patience, perserverence, and no small amount of humility. They will require networks of committed people and organizations who not only learn how to see the systems shaping how things work now, but also create alternatives.'
Peter Senge, business specialist (Note 17)

EXAMPLE: The global manufacturer of ecological cleaning products, Ecover, is a relatively small player in a highly competitive consumer goods market. Vital to its continued success is creating an open environment amongst stakeholders where sharing and collaboration is encouraged. It needs the collaborative assistance of its partners to drive innovation. For instance, in the development of its biodegradable bottles made from sustainably sourced sugar cane, collaboration is needed from parties involved in growing and harvesting through to research and development on package design. A new packaging process Ecover implemented with one supplier allowed distribution boxes to be folded and reused rather than destroyed and recycled. This system was later installed by the supplier across other organizations they also supplied, allowing the benefits to extend beyond Ecover's ecosystem while enhancing the resilience of its own ecosystem by helping its supplier provide additional systemic value. This collaboration extends to its customers too, and through social media Ecover has organized customer judging panels for new product ingredients and fragrances. Also, customers can test out new products, providing direct feedback while openly sharing this feedback with other customers. (Note 18)

The concept of stakeholder ecosystems in business has been around for some years, with large corporations like Cisco, Siemens and General Electric successfully building partner ecosystems to aid their performance. As the requirement for authenticity and transparency increases, so too does the need to connect and engage authentically with social and environmental stakeholder groups. Partnerships with local charities, community interest groups, NGOs and government institutions can help build this trust, break down historic barriers, help form working relationships and the mobilization of wider ranging resources which can enhance innovation and increase access to different skill types. It is important to invest time in getting to know these local groups, their activities, issues, areas of concern and tensions.

EXAMPLE: BC Hydro, a Canadian utility, developed a joint initiative between provincial governments in consultation with First Nation indigenous groups and the general public. This joint initiative offered a collaboration approach which enabled ecological wisdom to be integrated into business decision-making, leading to enhanced cross-cultural learning and improved outcomes for the overall ecosystem of partners. [Note 19]

EXAMPLE: IKEA, the well-known furniture manufacturer and distributor, successfully embarked on a 'Future Search' workshop to design a new global approach to product design, manufacturing and distribution. What usually would have taken months of complex systems design and rounds of sign-off and agreement, IKEA managed to do in three days. 58 stakeholders, decision makers and executives from around the world worked together in 18 hours of workshops. [Note 20] Expert facilitation was essential to helping guide the flow of the workshop which started by mapping out how things currently work and having multi-functional groups work through and agree on things. In this Future Search approach, any disagreements and conflicts are treated as information only rather than captured on action agendas. Common ground is sought and shared inspirations are encouraged. Different participants are invited to share challenges and specific market context perspectives. The groups work on gaining agreement to what has been mapped out, while starting to explore a new way beyond the challenges and problems of the current way. Letting go of the past can be difficult and getting people to work creatively together on different scenarios of the future can help transcend silos, allowing boundaries to permeate, and for people to start empathizing with different people's perspectives across the whole system.

Convivial evening dinners, creative activities, expert facilitation and pleasant comfortable surrounds help foster an atmosphere conducive to collaboration and exploration rather than 'them' and 'us' groups forming, while lifting the mood into a creative problem solving spirit. Energy for innovation and new ways of doing business can often buffer up against apprehensions of change, but gaining buy-in from different senior executives across the system helps alleviate some of this cynicism and suspicion of change.

Then the groups work on how the agreed new way can be implemented by the stakeholders, agreeing on how to coordinate post-workshop activity to build immediate momentum. In the case of IKEA, the new system was successfully agreed upon by all affected functions and a signed-off implementation plan achieved within the three days. Seven task forces were set up immediately and just a few days after the workshop the first cross-stakeholder meeting of a key customer, supplier and manufacturing team was held to start prototyping the new way.

This kind of intense systemic work allows an embodied experience of the whole system to form within each of the participants whereupon they can start to relate and empathize with other stakeholders more effectively with a shared level of respect and understanding. It leads to better working relations post-workshop and helps the success of the implementation plan. Rather than a 'one-off' intervention like this one at IKEA, how about we run regular Future Search workshops across our respective business ecosystems to allow for a continual prototyping, searching and empathizing to occur, synergizing deeper understanding about the challenges and opportunities arising in our ever-changing business context?

VALUES-LED

Values are like the nylon-string in the necklace holding everything together; a largely unseen organizational belief system, weaving through everything as the integrating factor in our teams and stakeholder groups. In a firm of the future, it is values, rather than control mechanisms, that ensure consistency of behavior in realizing the organization's mission.

The more we cultivate values-based decision-making in our teams, the more we create positive virtuous cycles by lessening the decisions and actions we take based on fear, separation and control; and the more we take decisions and actions that create futures which resonate with our deeper sense of purpose while enhancing our integrity and authenticity.

EXAMPLE: The American-based logistics and storage company, Container Store, is a perennial on 'Best Place to Work' lists, with consistent low staff turn-over and high morale, creativity and productivity. When hiring new employees, the company looks for good judgement and sound integrity above all else believing other skills can be taught. It spends time ensuring all new staff members immerse themselves in the company values and beliefs, and the way people treat and respect each other. This includes the way stakeholders of all shapes and sizes are engaged with. For instance, the company recently spent time with suppliers looking at creative ways to help its smaller

suppliers through the slow seasons so that they could avoid
having to lay off staff; hence building trust and reciprocity across
relations within and beyond organizational boundaries. [Note 21]

EXAMPLE: The Indian conglomerate, Tata Group, has a
longstanding commitment to enhancing all stakeholder relations
where possible. Tata's values are:

> INTEGRITY: We must conduct our business fairly, with
> honesty and transparency. Everything we do must stand
> the test of public scrutiny.

> UNDERSTANDING: We must be caring, show respect,
> compassion and humanity for our colleagues and
> customers around the world, and always work for the
> benefit of the communities we serve.

> EXCELLENCE: We must constantly strive to achieve the
> highest possible standards in our day-to-day work and in
> the quality of the goods and services we provide.

> UNITY: We must work cohesively with our colleagues
> across the group and with our customers and partners
> around the world, building strong relationships based on
> tolerance, understanding and mutual cooperation.

> RESPONSIBILITY: We must continue to be responsible,
> sensitive to the countries, communities and environments
> in which we work, always ensuring that what comes from
> the people goes back to the people many times over.

Tata is clear to point out that it is not business first and values
second, it is values that direct and shape business behavior. Yet
the Group would be the first to admit that this approach is a

journey of continuous learning and improvement with there being plenty of opportunities to do things better in the continual strive toward excellence. (Note 22)

For a firm of the future, the values of the organization attune with the value-creation objectives of the organization (social, environmental and economic); values and value reinforce each other and so a values-led culture drives the value-creation potential of the organization. The value-creation potential of the organization is realized for the short, medium and long term through a deep understanding of all relationships and resources within the organization and wider business ecosystem. Local attunement, agility, empowerment and creative freedom are governed by these values and the focus on value, not by hierarchical command-and-control. Some core values are listed here to act as a platform for debating values most appropriate for your organization:

- Recognition of interdependence

- Self-determination

- Diversity and tolerance

- Compassion for others

- Upholding the principle of equity

- Recognition of the rights and interests of non-humans

- Respect for the integrity of natural systems

- Respect for the interests of future generations [Note 23]

LIFE SUPPORTING

Sustainable business, sometimes called corporate social responsibility (CSR), has been around for a good few years now. To start with, for many organizations, it was often seen as a bolt-on to business-as-usual, a nice-to-have activity that could be dispensed with in times of downturn. But as systemic understanding of the challenges and opportunities of sustainable business has deepened a variety of organizations across all sectors are now seriously coming to terms with what it means to be sustainable. In the process, the term 'sustainability' has begun to evolve within some vanguard organizations and institutions. The terms 'flourishing', 'thriving' and 'net positive' are replacing 'sustainability'. Essentially, these new business terms refer to the organizational desire to go beyond merely managing and reducing the negative impacts of business operations (and also the wider value-chain and systemic socio-economic and ecological impacts directly or indirectly related to their business operations). It is pointing to a general shift in awareness toward what we call here 'regenerative business', whereupon we transcend yesterday's mechanistic logic by opening our personal and organizational awareness up to the deeper and wider wisdom inherent in life.

This shift from yesterday's linear logic to a deeper understanding of what it means to be a regenerative living business system immersed within the living systems of our society, economy and ecological world is a profound shift that is at the heart of this metamorphosis from a firm of the past to a firm of the future.

Such a shift is not for the faint hearted as it asks us, individually and organizationally, to question our dominant business assumptions and our sense of place and purpose in this world. The perfect storm of economic, social and environmental factors facing us demands nothing less of us.

'Life supporting' is about creating the conditions conductive for life in all aspects of our business activity; encouraging behaviors, products and services that enhance wellbeing not just for us but for the fabric of life. This is a quest, an exploration, an inquiry, in which we consistently hold close to our decision-making the question 'does this business initiative help create conditions conducive for life?' While we may feel in the short term this burdens us with additional responsibility, it actually opens up our perceptual horizon, encouraging us to work with stakeholders in deeper ways and in the process enriching our future through diversity, systemic thinking and reciprocating relations of synergy.

EXAMPLE: The global carpets manufacturer, Interface, has focused on reducing its negative impacts for many years now. Its Mission Zero strategy aims to have zero emissions (zero toxic pollutants in all solid, liquid and gas emissions across all its global operations) by 2020. It is on track to achieve this and in-so-doing has innovated new ways of operating that have improved its resilience.

As 2020 looms nearer, there have been conversations across the company about what lies beyond this Mission Zero goal. The question 'can we be life supporting?' has been explored at all levels of the organization sparking out-of-the-box creativity and a variety of innovative suggestions, strategies and pilot projects. By example, Net Works is a project that partners with an array of stakeholders in order to create conditions conducive for life. In working with local communities on Philippine islands, along with global and local charities, these communities have set up local banks, trading networks and capabilities to enable them to clean-up their polluted seas by gathering discarded fishing nets ready for processing into a form that can then be used by Interface for manufacturing carpet tiles. Clearly this has a beneficial effect on the marine environment, but also on the local communities. Recent tsunamis devastated much of the region but the communities engaged with the Net Works project were more resilient than other communities because of the local banks, exchanges and connections they put in place for the project.

EXAMPLE: Triodos is an international bank that aims to make money a force for good. Its core purpose as a business is to provide finance for enterprises that enhance quality of life through providing benefits to society and the environment. Unlike other international banks, there is total transparency for all stakeholders including the general public to see what Triodos is investing in and the conditions of borrowing for each and every investment. Triodos seeks to take a long term perspective in its investment decisions and where appropriate aims to form long term synergistic relations with its clients.

By way of example, one such project undertaken by Triodos UK is Golden Lane Housing (GLH). GLH is a housing associated with a mission to provide local housing for people with learning disabilities and mental health issues. Triodos first helped GLH raise finance through a bond issue ten years ago when GLH was just starting out. It actively kept in touch with GLH over the years, and two years ago helped with a larger bond raising venture enabling the now successful GLH to raise further funds for further expansion so that more local people who need it can benefit from local housing and social care.

Another example of a long term relationship is that of Jamie's Farm. A few years back, Triodos UK helped Jamie's Farm purchase its first 'care farm' with a mission of running week long programmes for adolescent children to help them break the self-destructive traps of anti-social behavior, delinquency and drug-abuse. After the initial purchase, Triodos kept in touch and provided assistance where it could, such as facilitating Jamie's Farm owners to connect with other care farms and international care farm networks. Following the success of the first farm, Triodos has recently helped Jamie's Farm purchase its second farm, enabling it to provide more benefit to more children.

EXAMPLE: The global retail group, Kingfisher, has a variety of homecare and DIY outlets throughout the world. The group has a business strategy of becoming net-positive across all its operations by 2050. This strategic intent has sparked much innovation and creative explorations across the business group. For instance, in the UK the outlet B&Q works collaboratively with local community groups providing DIY equipment for local hire. These 'Street Clubs' then foster reciprocity within the community with people interested in DIY using the pooled community tools to help others in the community with jobs, like putting up shelves, and in return people share other activities, like taking the kids to school or looking after an elderly neighbor. The communities flourish as these sharing connections foster better social relations, reciprocity, empathy and understanding across diverse communities. Where the Street Clubs flourish so too does the footfall in local B&Q outlets.

The transformation toward the firm of the future is a journey not a destination. These Business Principles help shape that journey, yet there is no ideal business model or perfect way of operating, more it is about finding the right way at the right time for the market conditions and organization's disposition.

Let's pause and reflect for a moment.

What could a firm of the future vision for your organization look like?

Spend a few moments pondering on this vision and start to imagine what the experience would be like to work in your regenerative firm of the future.

ADAPTIVE CYCLE OF LIVING SYSTEMS

Let's explore a bit more about what this innate regenerative logic within life looks and feels like, and how it can be applied to our organizations.

Scientific research into the dynamics of living systems has identified four distinct phases of development:

> growth (G)
>
> conservation (C or K)
>
> collapse or release (R or Omega)
>
> reorganization (O or Alpha)

In their pioneering work with the Resilience Alliance and in their book *Panarchy*, Lance H. Gunderson and C.S. Holling explore how these phases interact in living systems, including human organizations and communities. (Note 24) These phases form a continual looping round through a figure-of-eight cycle known as the 'adaptive cycle'. This oscillating creativity, conservation, breakdown and breakthrough occurs naturally in all living systems, including our organizations, through interacting cycles nested at different levels (space and time scales: localized or more regional, short-term or more long-term). (Note 25)

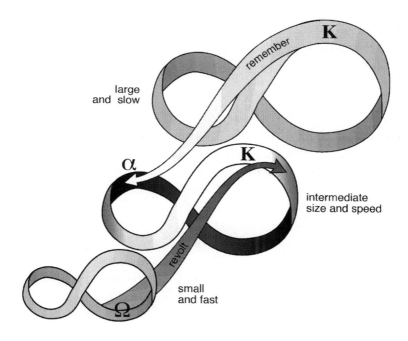

Figure 3-10

Image from Panarchy edited by Lance H. Gunderson and C.S. Holling. Copyright 2002 Island Press. Reproduced by permission of Island Press, Washington, DC.

The first and second phases of growth (G) and conservation (K) – referred to as the 'front loop' - represent growth through an incremental process of increasing efficiency, learning and innovation resulting in incremental changes toward a state of conservation. The third and fourth phases of collapse (Ω) and reorganization (α) – referred to as the 'back loop' - represent a disruption of this conservation stage as breakdown (Omega or death) in existing structures. In the midst of this breakdown, radically new ways of operating begin to emerge and breakthrough (Alpha or birth). This is the way of life: birth, growth, conservation and death leading to new birth, or spring shoots leading to summer growth then autumn harvests giving way to winter decay providing fertile soil for new shoots to take root once again; each season has its place in this cycle of life. (Note 26)

Cycles are nested and inter-related. For instance, a short localized cycle may interact with a short or long regional cycle. Hence, the two-way interaction between cycles represents the way living systems both persist (from memory of the large and slow) and yet innovate (from revolt of the small and fast). It shows how small and big, and fast and slow events and processes, can transform organizations through continuous cycles of creativity (both of incremental learning and radical innovation). (Note 27)

Knock-on effects of one cycle of transformation can influence another cycle, which can influence another, and so on. These adaptive cycles are present in our organizations at nested levels (individuals, teams, organization, wider business ecosystem, socio-economic system). It is through these phases that continuous adaptation, learning, renewal and reconfiguration occur. We pioneer a new product or service, launch it into the marketplace, fuel growth and gain market position through efficiencies and effectiveness, then market disturbances or inflection points mean a re-organization or reconfiguration is required.

Yesterday's logic tends to view development within a business unit or organization as linear: from innovation, launch and growth through to successful delivery of a profitable service. Once there, we feel we ought to hold tightly to a position of dominance repeating what we know works with incremental improvements and enhancements. Yet this one-way growth model misses out the important decline and breakdown stage (which is often viewed negatively by our dominant logic focused all-too narrowly on short-term profit maximization). The breakdown stage is the important back-loop that connects the cycle from growth and conservation to new innovations and re-growth – so essential for resilience in volatile market conditions.

In part, this back-loop reminds us of the importance of embracing failure as part of the innovation and growth cycle of any value-proposition, recognizing that we learn a great deal from working up prototypes that then need to be amended or redone in different ways; also the importance of having multiple value creation and delivery approaches for adapting to varying market conditions. Many Silicon Valley start-ups' ability to flourish is in part because of their tenacious ability to learn through failing, adapting quickly as they go. Yet, the wisdom of the adaptive-cycle also conveys a deeper recognition that business systems have an innate cyclic, spiraling, ebbing-and-flowing inter-relationality which pulsates with nested rhythms. This deeper recognition allows us to see beyond the superficiality of one-way growth models and narrowly focused business plans. Every value proposition is immersed within social, economic and ecological rhythms; the more we cultivate our multi-dimensional attunement of this inter-relationality the more regenerative our enterprises can become.

Former CEO of Mitsubishi, Tachi Kiuchi, and former President of Future 500, Bill Shireman, in their book *What We Learned In The Rainforest*, explore in detail the application of these ecological phases or 'seasons' in business: innovation, growth, improvement and release (reorganization). [Note 28] All the time different parts of the business will be in different phases. A flourishing future-fit organization is like a 'living laboratory' or diverse ecosystem with nested inter-related cycles all locally attuning, learning to feel what is an appropriate 'seasonal way of doing' for the business context and phase they are experiencing.

For instance, if our team or service area is in the reorganization and radical innovation phase, we let go of controlled outcomes while creatively prototyping, exploring our emerging future and selecting what works and what doesn't, trial through failing and learning, by embracing self-organizing team dynamics, envisioning, exploring and experimenting. Then, as we move into the 'growth' phase we bring in more of a 'project management' awareness to focus on operational issues, efficiencies, economies of scale, developing capacity through continuous improvements on quality, yet still keeping smaller nested cycles of prototyping and adapting within the larger, longer, slower gradient up into the growth phase. These smaller nested cycles bring in more variety and economies of scope to balance scale, with training in core skills being enriched with 'blue-sky' envisioning, insights into future business trends, and 'future search' workshops to start to prepare for the back-loop that lies beyond the front-loop currently being experienced.

Hence, we keep ourselves ever-ready to adapt and evolve as market conditions change while learning to sense when it's best to focus more on creative prototyping, more on project management or more on future-searching. Then the 'release' stage occurs when significant disruptions affect us, such as new technologies displacing current ways, new entrants competing in radically new ways, or radical shocks to market conditions. We enter a period of releasing and reallocating resources, reorganizing, re-envisioning and sensing new possibilities for innovation and investment. These ever-changing seasons of spring (innovation), summer (growth), autumn (consolidation), and winter (breakdown) are inherent in life; we ignore them at our peril, it's best to embrace them by continuously building in awareness of where we are at in the cycle.

There is a tendency in today's short-term mind-set to seek eternal summer moments, maximize the good times, in-so-doing abstracting ourselves from the inherent regenerative logic of living systems. This only leads to major swings of credit-fuelled, investment-light boom-and-bust bubbles which are not at all constructive for the overall health of the organization or wider socio-economic system. It is far wiser to learn to leverage the cycles our organization is both emanating and subject to, as this will greatly help our understanding of our internal and external dynamics of transformation and so help us navigate the inevitable yet unpredictable cycles of breakdown and breakthrough.

With this wisdom comes a deeper dawning realization within us personally, organizationally and culturally that both the breakdowns and breakthroughs are constructive for our wellbeing. Our organizations ought not to expend vital energy trying to control their environments, trying to resist any part of the adaptive cycle other than growth. This only wastes vital energy and slows down our ability to embrace transformation healthily. Of far greater use is enhancing our awareness and understanding of the dynamic environment (both inner and outer) we are operating in. The collapse of one aspect of our business can lead to the release of resources and energy to be channelled toward new innovations (the breakdown leading to a breakthrough). Failure is viewed as a learning that yields success.

Business models and business ecosystems that encourage inter-related parts to grow and collapse in line with their own 'contextual harmonics' gain greater strategic resilience. We learn to swim with the stream, to ride the waves and use the undercurrents; tuning into the harmonics of life while finding our organization's improvisational melody.

EXAMPLE: Nike has experienced periods of rapid growth interrupted with periods of flat or declining growth. It has lived and breathed the ecological succession stages and survived to tell the tale. The key to Nike's continued success has been its ability to learn and adapt as an organization. In the early 1980s it moved from growth phase to conservation then decline and reorganization. By the end of the early 1990s, Nike had reorganized into a decentralized, diverse, differentiated business. During the 1990s it again experienced succession through growth (sales from $2bn rose to $9bn) to decline, being hit by an external shock of exposure through internet activism about child labour in its factories. Nike positively adapted by admitting to the problem and radically improving ethical standards and approaches across its operations and supply chain. Adapting to feedback from its business environment has enabled Nike to be successful in weathering storms along its journey. Nokia on the other hand, had a great track record of adapting and evolving over the years from a paper mill to rubber boot manufacturer and car tyre maker to global telecommunications leader. Over the last few years, however, it allowed itself to get too fixated on short-term shareholder returns taking its eye off the need to continuously sense out, innovate and adapt to market conditions, and so failing to adequately deal with market disruptions from Apple and others, significantly losing market share for its mobile handhelds without suitable new innovations coming on stream fast enough.

EXAMPLE: The software company Autodesk has reviewed its core value proposition over the years while adapting to a fast-evolving market place. In the early 1990's it shifted from specializing in computer-aided design software for a narrow market of designers and architects by diversifying into the larger markets of manufacturing, construction, real estate and infrastructure business. As the industry started to rapidly change in the late 1990's Autodesk acquired Discreet Logic to bring in media and film expertise which enriched its existing business capabilities. Then, in the downturn of 2001, it focused on selling software by subscription as a service over set time periods with free upgrades and support, radically reconfiguring its business model while aligning itself to the direction of the market. This redesign in time of downturn enabled it to capitalize on the next phase of the cycle. Now, it provides specialist sustainability solutions for manufacturing and design and is an active player in the 'design-led' revolution by assisting in the development of new ways of working across complex business environments including social enterprises.

POIESIS

Life can be seen as a matrix of inter-related nested adaptive cycles continually breathing in and out, creating and decaying. This continual breakdown of one process informing the creation of another, with myriad nested cycles all informing each other, is what the German philosopher, Martin Heidegger, referred to as a 'bringing forth' or 'poiesis' as the fundamental creative dynamic of life.

For Heidegger, as we learn to open up to these spiraling vortices enriching our creative potential, we engage in a more authentic 'being in the world', a less egotistic and more soulful expression of our selves. It is this 'bringing forth', or unfolding self-expression of our authenticity through our interactions with the world that is a fundamental dynamic of our self-actualization.

This is what is meant here by 'poiesis': our unfolding self-expression within the work we do. (Note 29)

Each of us personally experiences these adaptive-cycle stages - unfolding, inspiring, learning and developing - during continual phases of breakdown and breakthrough in our lives. Each cycle opening us up to deeper unfolding and learning as we go through a 'letting go', painful suffering and psychical release in order to make way for our deeper authenticity, inner truth and soulful sense of purpose to shine through. These phases of mini-death and rebirth cycles within our psyche are vital for our deeper 'bringing forth' of our authentic selves into our purposeful work. Our ego may attempt to prevent the mini-deaths and rebirths we experience within this unfolding venture, as they are painful and threatening to our current sense of self, yet if we are to open up to the regenerative reality of real life beyond the artificial yet comfortable confines of our ego, we ought learn to embrace these natural cycles for what they are.

In short, we are destined to live lives full of ups and downs, along with clarity and confusion; learning to see the polarities of 'good times' and 'bad times' within this cyclic context helps us constructively cope with these 'swings and roundabouts'.

From a psychological perspective, our conscious mind is reliant upon the unconscious psyche for its fuller expression. It is these turbulent eddies and under-currents that challenge our daily awareness with darkness, suffering and psychical release from the depths beneath our superficial ego-persona. And so our daily ego-consciousness is reliant on deeper regenerative cycles for its fuller expression. Carl Jung explored this journey of self-actualization and saw how fundamental this spiraling churning conscious-unconscious tension is to our overall psychological health, vitality and development. He once famously said, 'There is no coming to consciousness without pain. People will do anything, no matter how absurd, in order to avoid facing their own Soul. One does not become enlightened by imagining figures of light, but by making the darkness conscious.'

The more conscious we learn to become of our own rhythms and cycles of psychological growth and renewal, the more effective we are as leaders and change agents. There is evidence that points to personal transformation cycles tending to follow an approximate seven yearly cycle. Within these cycles there are yearly, seasonal and lunar (moon) cycles all inter-relating with bio-rhythms within us. (Note 30)

By sensing how we are really feeling beneath the distracting cacophony of the everyday, we can sense when we may need to take time to renew ourselves. Rather than allowing ourselves to become increasingly agitated, restless, impatient and forceful or oversensitive, depressive, unsure, defensive and withdrawn, we have the courage and self-determination to take time out, to sense inwardly, rejuvenate and find a more coherent and balanced state of awareness. This way we can ensure we allow a more creative, vitalizing, convivial and compassionate awareness to flow through our relations and interactions. This is a process of 'self-mastery' and part-and-parcel of this is to intimately sense when we need to take appropriate action to pause, rest, reflect, renew, so that we heal in a deeply rejuvenating way as opposed to applying proverbial Band Aids which do not give adequate space for deeper reflection and renewal.

> 'This above all: to thine own self be true.'
> *Shakespeare, playwright*

At a collective level, the more our organizational culture is able to sense the swings of these nested cycles, embracing the learnings they yield, then the more creative and wise the organizational psyche becomes, deepening its collective cultivation of its 'being-in-the-world' as an organizational living system.

A continual learning environment that allows for plenty of space to reflect, discuss and share constructive feedback is important here, as is embracing the techniques of deep listening, sharing circles (for example, Way of Council or Story Café discussed later), gatherings with no agenda, group sessions away from the office, and artful interventions at different points within the cycle.

Our own adherence to the regenerative rhythms of life is what helps ensure our organization's regenerative logic is continuously enlivened. By creating space in our schedules to reflect, let go and explore our learning, suffering and vulnerability, we allow for deeper, more authentic expressions of our self and our teams to create new ways out of the ashes of the old. In fact, let's go into our diaries, right now, and block out at least one two-hour slot each week for reflection and renew.

Artful expressions, intuitions, imaginative explorations, envisioning, deep listening and soulful sharing at every stage of our journey helps us, our teams and organizations transform fears, tensions, failures and conflict into deeper learning, authenticity, creativity and resilience.

And I know one thing.
We are not born to avoid dying by lying low and playing safe.
We are born to live.
We are born to leave the garden more beautiful than we found it.
Mac Macartney, leadership specialist (Note 31)

REFLECTIVE QUESTIONS

How would you describe your organization's current mission, sense of purpose and strategic intent? Does it primarily focus on financial value or is there serious intent to also create social and ecological value?

Bearing in mind the state of the world today and the ever-deepening inter-related nature of the social, ecological and economic problems we face, do you feel the organization you dedicate your time and energy to ought to have a strategic intent that is more closely aligned to regenerative business?

Imagine your company becoming a firm of the future. How do you feel about working for a company that is seeking to become regenerative? Do you feel inspired, committed, determined to make a success of your contribution to this organization's journey toward regenerative business? Imagine all your colleagues also feeling this way, what creative energy and passion would that unleash?

Can you imagine what our global economy as a whole would look like if all companies (or atleast the majority of them) strived to become regenerative? Would this seem like a more suitable kind of world for our children to inherit rather than the one we are currently leaving them?

What about if every organization was measured against a future-fit benchmark, that measured and rewarded those that will positively shape our future? (Note 32)

MODULE **THREE**

SHIFTING THE LOGIC

SHIFTING OUR INGRAINED
ACCULTURATED LOGIC BOTH
PERSONALLY AND ORGANIZATIONALLY
IS NO MEAN FEAT. THE GOOD NEWS IS
THAT THIS SHIFT IS NOTHING MORE AND
NOTHING LESS THAN AN OPENING UP
TO WHO WE TRULY ARE, RESULTING IN
MORE ALIVE, CREATIVE, CONVIVIAL,
COMPASSIONATE ENTERPRISES.

EXECUTIVE SUMMARY

- A number of well-researched developmental models detail progressive stages of personal consciousness.

- At a certain point in our psychological development there is a moment of personal transformation or self-actualization involving a breaking-down of our old mind-set hand-in-hand with a breaking-through of new perspectives: a fundamental transfiguration of our sense of place and purpose in the world.

- Each of us has an ego-soul dynamic within us, a set of forces which on the one hand (the ego) clings to safety and defensiveness out of fear and separation afraid to jeopardize the status quo sense of self; on the other hand (the soul) impels us to grow, to develop toward a deeper uniqueness, confidence, openness and compassion in the face of the world.

- As we self-actualize we learn to cultivate the ego-soul dynamic within our psyche.

- This self-actualization comes with a more coherent perspective that embraces all of our natural ways of knowing: intuitive, rational, sensorial and emotional.

- This more coherent personal perspective helps us engage and relate in ways that catalyze our organizational journey toward a regenerative firm of the future.

'WITHOUT A GLOBAL REVOLUTION IN
THE SPHERE OF HUMAN
CONSCIOUSNESS THE CATASTROPHE
TOWARD WHICH THE WORLD IS HEADED
WILL BE UNAVOIDABLE.'

VACLAV HAVEL, PRIME MINISTER, ADDRESSING
US CONGRESS

MANY GREAT MINDS HAVE SPENT significant time and effort rigorously exploring the ways we relate as leaders and team members, along with our ethics, values and behaviors in our organizations. Here we provide a synopsis of the key aspects of this research before diving in to a deeper exploration of the 'ways of being' needed to underpin and infuse the 'ways of doing' we explored in the last module.

A good place to start is Abraham Maslow's famous 'hierarchy of needs' published in 1943, which describes the psychological stages our human motivations move through: physiological (essential metabolic needs of food and water, clothing and shelter), safety (personal and economic security, general health and wellbeing), love and belonging (the need to be involved in emotional and intimate relations), self-esteem (feeling valued by others, self-confidence and a feeling of independence), self-actualization (the actualization of our creative, embodied potential through what we do, whereupon we begin to bring all our natural ways of knowing into alignment. Within the upper part of this self-actualization stage is self-transcendence - the realization of our deeper soul-calling by being in service to something greater than ourselves). [Note 1]

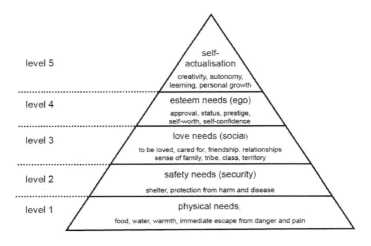

Image from Abraham Maslow, Motivation & Personality, 1sr Ed., Copyright 1970. Reprinted by permission of Pearson Education, Inc., New York.

The last few decades have born witness to the general application of a number of developmental psychology models for organizational leadership. A couple worth mentioning here are William Torbert's action logic levels of consciousness applied to business leaders; Jean Gebster's Integralism followed by Ken Wilber's Integral Theory and Jenny Wade's application of this for optimizing organizational cultures and structures; Clare Graves', Don Beck's and Christopher Cowan's Spiral Dynamics theory applied to levels of consciousness in human cultures, organizations and leadership styles; the well-received recent study by Frederic Laloux on Evolutionary-Teal organizational cultures and structures (drawing on Spiral Dynamics and Integral Theory); Richard Barrett's seven levels of consciousness for leaders and organizations. (Note 2)

All these developmental models detail progressive stages of consciousness – by 'consciousness' we mean our awareness, how we relate and engage with ourselves and others in our organizations. The originators and practitioners of these models are keen to point out that as individuals and groups of people (teams, organizations and wider networks of stakeholders) we 'transcend and include' these levels of consciousness as we progress, i.e. as we advance in conscious awareness we contain within us the awareness of the lower levels while enriching our perceptual horizon with a deepening consciousness that transforms how we view our selves and the world around us.

All these developmental models point to a threshold being crossed at a certain level, where a major shift from ego-orientated consciousness transcends into a state where our 'ego-awareness' and 'soul-awareness' permeate more readily, infusing into a more integrated, inclusive and holistic awareness. In Maslow's hierarchy this threshold is crossed from the level of self-esteem into the level of self-actualization and self-transcendence. This is a fundamental transformation of our sense of place and purpose in the world. As our ego-self begins to permeate we open up to more of reality beyond the narrowing sense of the ego. We begin to become conscious of the inter-relational nature of our human systems and more-than-human world.

This integrated ego-soul awareness is inclusive of the previous levels of consciousness. Multiple intelligences work and combine together rather than trying to vie for dominance. It is here that a multi-dimensional consciousness of 'inter-being' emerges [Note 3], and we find our natural capacity to deal creatively, compassionately and authentically in complex, ever-changing environments. This level of consciousness comes with a felt-sense of embodied knowingness, a heightened state of presence, and a sense of calmness even amid great turmoil. This state has been referred to as being 'in the flow' or 'in the zone' by leaders, athletics and artists alike.

Throughout the immense wealth of contemporary research on organizational leadership now available, a consistent theme shines through: leaders' personal effectiveness and organizations' resilience are directly proportional to the inner-awareness (or 'level of consciousness') of the leaders, managers and team players involved in strategic decisions and day-to-day operations. It may sound a bit trite or perhaps rather obvious to point this out, yet this fundamental issue is often overlooked, or paid mere lip-service, in many of today's mainstream methods of organizational strategy and operations.

In our rush to find techno-fixes to our present day problems we so often end up reinforcing the level of consciousness that created our problems in the first place. We apply an ego-dominated mechanistic awareness to drive through change, in-so-doing we leave the fundamentals unchanged and so problems persist, spreading deeper and wider in their ramifications. Hence, our ability to understand, embody, practice and cultivate our awareness is core to our becoming future-fit. In other words, our 'ways of doing' manifest successfully only if underpinned and infused by 'ways of being'.

Before we explore the what-and-how of cultivating this enhanced consciousness, it is worth saying a few words about the two phrases 'ego-awareness' and 'soul-awareness' in terms of how they are used in this workbook.

Sigmund Freud defined the ego as a 'reality function' in that it brings our awareness into the sharper space-time dimension from the more intangible, fluid depths of the largely unconscious imaginal realms, where the soul, as the source of our essence, resides. (These largely unconscious realms are where the energetic and quantum dimensions of reality pervading our psychical world reside, always present within and all around us yet lying outside the perceptual horizon of our daily consciousness awareness).

The ego creates an encapsulated sense of self as separate from the otherwise fluid, connective and inter-relational world we inhabit. It creates a marked-out territory of 'self' that is fenced-off from the world, in-so-doing it creates a sense of separation from the world. This sense of separation heightens through fear as we sense a need to defend ourselves from a hostile world while attempting to protect, enhance and maximize 'self' as separate from 'other'.

The ego undertakes an important moderating function for us, moderating what we take into our field of conscious awareness, filtering through perspectives and judgements of what is useful or what ought to be resisted. An ego that is too rigid or impermeable prevents our self-development by restricting too much of our immediate domain through excessive judging, filtering and objectifying. Likewise, an ego that is too easily overwhelmed by experience cannot adequately integrate the experience into our conscious awareness and daily functioning.

A well-developed ego-awareness is needed in today's and tomorrow's organizations. The only problem with our ego-awareness is that it has a tendency to dominate, due to its incessant grasp gripping tighter in moments of uncertainty, dislocating 'present' from 'past' and 'future' in order to critique 'what is' and make plans for 'what isn't yet'.

It can become self-fuelling in its search for a problem to solve. Past learning becomes burdened with guilt and future planning burdened with worry and over-analysis. If our ego-awareness is left unchecked it soon becomes a continual stream of mental chatter which breeds and recycles anxiety, narrowing down our attention in a way that induces profound psychic suffering, reducing our capacity for empathy and heightening our competitiveness through a narrowed-down perspective of 'I' in competition with others. This fuels anxiety and over-analysis, exacerbating a dis-embodied perspective which dis-locates us from our own life-force while strangling our conscious ability to readily engage with our embodied emotions, intuitions and soulful depths - the very ways of knowing we depend on to enrich our spontaneity, aliveness, creativity and ability to deal with change. And so a dis-eased state ensues; a sense of lack and scarcity creeps in as a result of this dis-embodied awareness. Our attitude of mind becomes one of 'having', 'wanting', 'owning', 'consuming'. In our desire to grasp ever-tighter on to certainty and control due to our increasing anxiety, we find it more and more difficult to deal with complex emergent situations with 'out-of-the-box' thinking. We become caught up in the very thinking that created our problems in the first place, becoming trapped in our own delusion of consciousness. (Note 4)

So, the challenge for each of us is to learn how to tame this tenacious ego-awareness of ours so that we are able to utilize its usefulness without allowing it to undermine our greatness. We must learn to detect when this grasping tendency starts to grip us, and learn how to ease its grip, so we can be masters of our own ego-awareness, rather than it dominating and closing us off from who we truly are.

The soul is our true nature; the deeper essence of who we are (what Carl Jung referred to as the 'Self'). This Self is ever-present and underlies the masks, personas and projections created by our ego. Yet, for much of our waking lives, we obscure this deeper authentic presence with our ego-chatter, projections and judgements. As we learn to tame our ego, we also learn to allow more of our natural soul-awareness to permeate through into our daily consciousness.

Abraham Maslow noted that each of us has an ego-soul dynamic within us, a set of forces which on the one hand - the ego - likes clinging to safety and defensiveness out of fear and separation, afraid to jeopardize the status quo sense of self; on the other hand - the soul - impels us to grow, to develop toward a deeper uniqueness, toward greater confidence in the face of the world, to accept more of the unconscious depths within and around us. In Maslow's words, 'This basic dilemma or conflict between the defensive forces and the growth trends I conceive to be existential, imbedded in the deepest nature of the human being, now and forever into the future.' (Note 5) It is this tension between the clinging nature of our ego-defences and the expansive deepening nature of our soul-wisdom that we refer to here in this workbook as the 'ego-soul dynamic'.

Richard Barrett explores this ego-soul dynamic through his seven stages of psychological development: surviving, relating, differentiating, transformation, internal cohesion, making a difference, and service. As we develop through these stages we deepen in our understanding, awareness and choice of growth over security. We learn to develop an ego-soul dynamic within our daily consciousness that allows for more of 'who we truly are' to inform how we perceive and relate during our working day (and personal life in general). We become more soulful in learning to open up our perspective beyond the narrowing frames of our ego-masks, and in-so-doing, we enrich our decisions, actions and relations for the benefit of our team, organization and stakeholders. We transcend the logic that created the problems in the first place and deal with our challenges at their root.

To summarise, the ego provides us with a sense of 'I' which we need for functioning in the world, but if it becomes too dominant, it fills us with a sense of heightened separation from the world, along with a feeling of being innately in competition with others while continuously struggling for survival in a hostile world; soon an anxious, grasping, stress-inducing, fearful perspective inflates within us, which seeks to dominate, blame, project, judge, manipulate, exploit and control rather than our opening up creatively and compassionately to what is emerging in our experience of life.

The soul, on the other hand, deeply understands the inter-relationality of life, the inherent physical and psychical, electromagnetic and quantum, all-pervasive matrix of reality within which our lives operate (largely beyond the confines of our ego-world). While the ego senses separation, fear, control and scarcity; the soul senses abundance, inter-being, flourishing and creativity within the unceasing change and uncertainty of a wild yet wonderfully enchanting world. While the ego seeks survival, security and maximization of the individual self through management, control and exploitation of the world around it, the soul seeks a purpose-driven life in service of something greater than the individual self. Yet, the soul needs the ego for the manifestation of this purpose-driven life. And so it is an internal cohesion (or rather, a marriage, communion, alchemy or interplay) of the ego and soul that allows for the soul to realize its potential through us, hence the energetic relationship of our ego-awareness and soul-awareness within us is what we are seeking to cultivate: our ego-soul dynamic.

Richard Barrett's Seven Levels Model looks at psychological development through the lens of this ego-soul evolutionary dynamic: the motivations and development of the ego and the subtle influences of the soul in our journey of self-actualization and self-transcendence. (Note 6)

Stages in the Development of **Personal** Consciousness

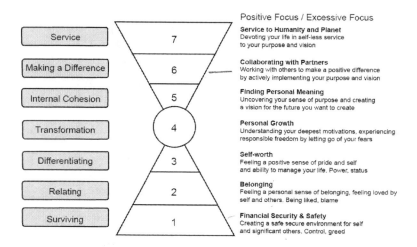

Image reproduced with permission from The Barrett Values Centre

In this diagram, it is level four 'Transformation' (also referred to as 'Individuating') where we begin to consciously cultivate a permeating of our ego-awareness with our soul. This is what Otto Scharmer from MIT has referred to in his Theory U as a 'letting go' to 'let come' whereupon we face-up to, challenge and transcend our long-held beliefs, mental habits and acculturations as we open up to the depths of our psyche with an open mind, open heart and open will. (Note 7) This letting go to let come can be a painful time of mixed highs and lows as old constructs are laid bare for what they are - self-illusions and artificialities we have created to prop up our ego-self's sense of persona, power, control and status. A mid-life crisis, a period of depression, sudden loss of status or an inner calling may provoke us to take a long hard look at ourselves, what some have called 'the dark night of the soul', which can last for months or years.

We start to cultivate our inner-awareness through personal practices, conscious learning and self-reflection. We begin to alchemize and reconfigure the behaviors, thought-patterns and habituations of the ego with the values of the soul. For instance, we may begin to recognize how sustainable business initiatives at work align with our deeper soul-sense and also bring in more innovative, creative, passionate 'out-of-the-box' ways of being and doing into our workplace.

This continues into the next stage of 'Internal Cohesion' (also referred to as 'Self-Actualizing') where we begin to come to terms with our ego-soul consciousness as we become more adept at aligning our different ways of knowing (intuitive, emotional, sensorial and rational) into our everyday living while dis-entangling ourselves from old habits. Our ego starts to learn how to embrace the interests and passions of the soul through a healthy, constructive style of leading and living within a values-led purpose-driven work-life. This allows for a deeper emergence of 'who we truly are' to come through us in our deepening authenticity, transparency, inter-relations, communications, continuous learning and self-recognizing. Life starts to be seen for what it really is, a rich 'action research' or 'collaborative inquiry' of learning as we go, exploring and deepening our sense of who we are while allowing more of our soul to emerge through us.

With this often comes a change in career path along with an awakening to a soul-calling as a clearer sense of purpose forms for us, beckoning us to make a difference in the world. And so in the 'Making a Difference' stage (also referred to as 'Integrating') we align our work-life (and way of living in general) more comprehensively as this deeper soul-calling emerges through us. This further enriches and transforms how we relate to others and serve the world. Then in the 'Service' stage of our development, we are fulfilling our destiny by aligning our lives to our soul's calling, being in service of what the soul informs us to do and allowing it to navigate us within an ever-changing context. This soul-calling orientates around being in service of the general wellbeing of Life in a way that relates to our unique strengths, passions and insights we bring to bear through our lives.

> 'Let the spirit world
> Come into passion
> Let the space of stillness
> Move us through our lives.'
> *Stephen K. Levine, psychotherapist* (Note 8)

Our ego's urge to dominate is ever-present and requires practice, patience and determination to tame. The more we practice the easier it becomes for this 'shift' into a more cohesive ego-soul dynamic to occur amid stressful situations, and life is always providing fresh challenges and opportunities for our ego-soul dynamic to attune with. It's an unfolding dance of authenticity, as we learn to infuse more of our soul into our creative endeavor, stumbling and struggling amid brief moments of dancing in soul-bliss.

The front-line of this work is our practical application through our everyday living and leading. And as we are creatures of cultural habit with collective behavioral patterns, institutionalized education systems, and mainstream socio-economic pathways all steeped in yesterday's logic, it is not an easy undertaking, and certainly not a viable path for the faint-hearted. Learning through failing, dogged experimentation and exploration, underpinned with courage and determination is what is required as we 'transcend and include', in-so-doing liberating and enriching ourselves and our organizations.

In the next two modules we look at practical ways we can help this ego-soul dynamic develop within our daily consciousness making for better leaders, teams and organizations. Now, we shall touch on some important explorations into our different ways of attending to reality, so that we can then later embrace practical techniques that draw on these findings in helping our personal and organizational development.

EMBRACING A FUNDAMENTAL SHIFT IN KNOWING

The pioneering psychologist Carl Jung explored our four natural ways of knowing as: thinking (rational analytical thought); feeling (emotional feelings); sensing (somatic embodied awareness); and psychical intuitions. The sweet spot is found when all these ways of knowing are working together rather than vying for control or trying to suppressing one another. In today's business world too much emphasis is placed on rational analytical thought at the expense of our other ways of knowing. Albert Einstein hit the nail on the head when he said, 'The intuitive mind is a sacred gift, the rational mind its faithful servant. We have created a society that honors the servant and has forgotten the gift.' [Note 9] We have created organizations that are so caught up the analytical, linear, reductive logic of our head thinking ego-mind that we have crowded out all our other ways of knowing and strangled our potential for ego-soul cohesion.

4 natural Ways of Knowing:

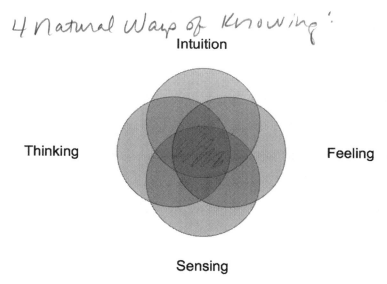

Image reproduced with permission from Simon Robinson and Maria Moraes Robinson co-authors of Holonomics (2014)

'Attention is a moral act: it creates, brings aspects of things
into being, in doing so makes others recede. What a thing
is depends on who is attending to it and in what way.'
Iain McGilchrist, neuroscientist

Neuroscientist Iain McGilchrist has extensively explored how
different ways of knowing relate in part to how our
bi-hemispheric brain works. Our bi-hemispheric brain enables us
to attend to the world with seemingly incompatible types of
attention at the same time: an open, inter-relational and
embodied way (right hemisphere) as well as a narrow, focused,
fragmenting and abstract way (left hemisphere). (Note 10) We need
both these ways of attending to perform effectively in business.

The narrowing-down, categorizing, atomizing focus of the left
hemisphere is what allows us to create the to-do lists, get-the-
job done, manage and control our time and resource budgeting,
engineer the nuts-and-bolts of our machines, models and
metrics. It is the left hemisphere that applies the intuitions,
feelings and insights of the right hemisphere into our practices,
products and processes. It is the right hemisphere that allows us
to deal with ever-changing dynamics and complex systems of
inter-relations, to see the wider context of situations, to
empathize and commune with others in a heartfelt way, and to
bring a more embodied soulful perspective into our awareness.
When our conscious awareness is primarily in our right
hemisphere, we open ourselves up to the full array of
kinaesthetic felt-senses of our sensitive bodymind - our sensorial,
intuitive and emotional ways of knowing.

Our right hemisphere sees things as they are: unfolding,
emergent, psychical and physical inter-relating systems of people
within teams within organizations within stakeholder
ecosystems within wider social systems within the

more-than-human systems of life on Earth, all nested within the quantum systems of this Universe. Our left hemisphere is constantly re-presenting this richly textured inter-relational matrix of reality through a rationalizing, objectifying perspective that separates continua into either/or polarities, creates categories and silos, quantifies and metricizes, manages and controls, and seeks to clearly define relationships as point-to-point trade-offs between neatly defined units. In its desire to 'make sense' of our world, the left hemisphere creates abstractions and objectifications that are, at best, approximations and assumptions filtered through learning and experience. Sometimes, these abstractions unwittingly de-sensitise and dis-embody our awareness from the very world we are wishing to make sense of; hence, the importance of re-balancing our left hemisphere's abstractions with the real world of the right.

In a healthy inter-hemispheric relation, we are continuously oscillating between the real-life insight or the right hemisphere (and the embodied soulful perspectives it draws on) and our re-presentation of it by the left; allowing us to be both creatures of distance, making projections about past learnings or future plans, while simultaneously immersed in the flow of life as-it-is. How amazing! There is a problem however. According to McGilchrist and other renowned experts in this field, the left hemisphere, with its grasping narrowing-down perspective, has a tendency to dominate, crowding out the right hemisphere, to the extent that we can get caught up in the abstractions of the left: we re-present what we have already re-presented without enriching it with the more embodied, intuitive, empathic and inter-relational perspective of the right. We get caught up in a hall of mirrors of our own abstractions – enter Einstein's optical delusion of consciousness.

Left hemisphere dominance has roots in a reductionist philosophy which came long before today's prevailing business

paradigm. Descartes and Newton, amongst others helped
nurture the age old seeds of reductionism: the view that the
behavior of the whole system can be explained in terms of the
behavior of its constituent parts. This atomization of complex,
interconnected systems has greatly assisted our modern scientific
research and development of technologies providing immense
benefit for us today. Management and monitoring approaches
have brought great strides in efficiency of operations, aiding our
understanding of the sub-system parts of business, and helping
us to analyze, quantify and control in intricate intelligent ways.
However, a focus on measuring atomized parts of the system
needs to be adequately balanced with an understanding of the
interconnected nature of business. For instance, key performance
indicators (KPIs) are useful for trend analysis and helping
identify areas that need our attention; though we need to be
conscious of the limitations and potential distortions these
numbers create in linearizing what are the non-linear inter-
relational dynamics of complex and emergent business systems.

The last decade or so has seen a marked increase in neuroscience
research findings related to our different ways of relating in
business, enriching our models of developmental psychology,
behavioral dynamics, organizational management and leadership.
For instance: Dr. J. Andrew Armour's neuro-cardiology research
explores the power of the heart as a neural network; Dr Candice
Pert's advancements in neuroscience through the discovery of
opiate receptors and the role of neuropeptides on our emotions
throughout our body, along with her conceptualization of the
'bodymind' – our mind resides throughout our body, and also
beyond it through its reverberation with our environment, it
does not reside solely in the brain; psychiatrist Dan Siegel's
research into the power of our attention in shaping our neural
networks and processing patterns; Dr Rollin McCraty and
others at The HeartMath Institute researching the centering

effect of heart-awareness on our overall consciousness and hemispheric-brain activity; neurobiologist Dr. Michael Gershon's research into the gut as a neural network with inherent learning, memory and complex processing capability; Professor George Lakoff and Dr Mark Johnson's research into human cognition originating from and contributing to embodied physical experience.

In a nut shell, we are now waking up to the realization that the human 'mind' has (at least) three 'brains' within it (head, heart and gut), all connected within a network of nerves, hormones, chemicals, sensory glands and electromagnetic and quantum fields resonating throughout our bodies and wider neighborhood.

Leadership and organizational specialists Grant Soosalu and Marvin Oka have explored the importance of listening to and engaging our three brains: head, heart and guts. In what they call mBIT 'multiple Brain Integration Techniques', drawn from behavioral modelling and neuroscience research, they explore how 'generative wisdom' forms when we bring our head, heart and gut awareness into alignment. [Note 11] These three areas in our body provide quite different feelings, perspectives and specialist ways of processing our lived experiences.

The more conscious we are of these three cognitive channels, the more we can call upon their different perspectives and align them in to our sensing and responding. Learning to tune-in to our subtle sensing and processing of our world as situations unfold greatly enhances our 'generative wisdom' – the way we experience, learn and participate in the unfolding dynamic of life. This makes for future-fit leadership, enhanced team dynamics, richer stakeholder relations and a more conscious organizational culture.

As we learn to cohere our different ways of knowing, we learn to transform how we experience reality; becoming consciously aware of, and learning to let go of, habituated perspectives and out-dated mind-sets. This helps us open up to more of reality beyond self-imposed limitations, learning from how we sense and respond to what life throws at us; transforming with each step as we go, while making mistakes, experiencing set-backs, failures, joyful moments; sensing what it feels like to be coherent as well as uncentered, authentic as well as inauthentic, and wise as well as superficial in our way of attending.

> 'Knowledge comes from but a single perspective; wisdom comes from multiple perspectives.'
> *Gregory Bateson, cyberneticist and social ecologist*

With practice, we can learn to cohere our three 'brains' amid stressful and challenging situations, allowing a rich concoction of intuitive, emotional, sensorial and rational messages to spark off each other and synchronize, rather than one way of knowing drowning out other insightful signals.

Oxford University practitioners Danah Zohar and Ian Marshall have explored our different types of knowing in terms of IQ, EQ and SQ (or 'quantum intelligence'). They have detailed how these ways of knowing draw from cognition, perception, intuition and sensation from our body and beyond. The analytical reasoning and meaning-making of our head-brain's cerebral cortex is largely IQ; EQ is the emotional awareness that originates beyond the head-brain in the heart region as well the instinctive perturbations of the gut and the wider neural, hormonal and nerve nets throughout our body's soma; SQ is our spiritual, intuitive, visionary awareness which emerges from a deeper coherence of consciousness throughout all regions of the body and beyond into a wider background ocean of consciousness (an electromagnetic and quantum field) within which we are immersed. (Note 12)

All the time more evidence is emerging across multiple disciples – for instance, neurology, developmental psychology, facilitation ecology, evolutionary biology and quantum physics – pointing to the existence of a 'field' of consciousness pervading the fabric of our lives and our wider universe. (Note 13) Through contemplative and reflective practices we can enhance how our daily consciousness tunes-in to this deeper all-pervasive field, in-so-doing opening ourselves up to richer wisdom beyond what our rationalizing ego-consciousness can grasp at.

> 'Our normal waking consciousness, rational consciousness
> as we call it, is but one special type of consciousness,
> whilst all about it, parted from it by the filmiest of screens,
> there lie potential forms of consciousness
> entirely different.'
> *William James, philosopher and psychologist*

The more we allow ourselves to attune with this 'field', the more coherent is our IQ, EQ and SQ, enhancing our ability to deal with the challenging situations unfolding in our midst; and the more effective, vital, creative, authentic and resilient we become.

This led the internationally-acclaimed neuroscientist and pharmacologist Candace Pert to coin the phrase 'bodymind', as it is the entire human body and its continuous inter-relationality within the ocean of electromagnetic and quantum fluctuations of this all-pervasive 'field' that forms our 'mind'. It is what the social ecologist and cyberneticist Gregory Bateson alluded to when referring to an Ecology of Mind, a sea of inter-relations all contributing to the Mind of Nature within which our minds are nested. As the quantum explorer Nassim Haramein aptly notes, 'looking for consciousness in the brain is like looking inside a radio for the announcer.' The more we become conscious of this inter-relationality within and all around us, the more we begin to perceive life beyond the mechanistic objects and separating silos of our over-active left-brained ego-awareness. We allow our sense of self to permeate with a deeper sense of inter-being, belongingness and meaning in our lives. This is a profound yet subtle shift in consciousness from an overly dominant ego-logic to a more soul-infused way of attending to ourselves, each other and the world around us.

The importance of all these findings for ourselves as leaders, and our organizations as collectives of conscious people, is simply this: the more we align our natural ways of knowing within us, the more able we are to help our organizations flourish in the ever-changing business context we now face. And we can start by allowing the natural capacities we have all been born with to see the light of day through practice and patience while learning to loosen the grip of our dominating ego-awareness.

The greatest obstacle to this subtle shift in consciousness is our selves: our own fears, habituated patterns of thought, and acculturated busyness. Much of our working life is driven by the impulse to be busy, to get things done. Getting things done is important, yet if we are doing things in a stressful, ego-dominated 'old logic' way, we apply the very same thinking to our well-intended solutions that created our problems in the first place.

> 'All of humanity's problems stem from man's inability to
> sit quietly in a room alone.'
> *Blaise Pascal, mathematician and philosopher*

Our busyness is an emotional dis-ease, a form of neurosis where we find it more comfortable to get busy than to be still for a moment. It is the stillness beneath the noisy notes within our hectic schedules that we need to tune into if we are to invite in our soul-awareness. Inviting in soul-awareness while learning to tame our ego amid our busy work schedules is what this workbook is all about, and so a number of 'tips' are provided throughout these pages to help us learn to cultivate soul spaces, reflective moments and bodymind coherence so that our 'ways of being' infuse our 'ways of doing'. This is what lies at the heart of becoming future-fit.

On that note, let's pause for a moment, and breathe deep.

> 'Don't just do something, sit there.'
> *Buddhist proverb*

Let's bring our awareness to ourselves reading this book, sense our surroundings, sense our breathing and our body posture. Let's get comfortable, take a couple of deep breaths, or if our situation allows, make a cuppa, stretch our legs, or even venture outside for a breath of fresh air.

When we feel ready, let's settle down comfortably, ready to explore our first tip to becoming future-fit.

TIP

CONSCIOUS BREATHING

The simple act of being conscious of our breathing can bring about a profound shift within us, as it can allow for coherence of our head, heart and gut.

It does not matter if we are standing in a queue, sitting at our desk, or sitting in a meeting, we can learn to practice conscious breathing where-ever and whenever, doing it discretely if we do not wish to bring attention to ourselves while we are doing it. All we are practicing is counting in our heads while we breathe in and out and also learning to sense the feeling between the in-breath and out-breath. Here are two simple techniques: the four-fold breath and sine-wave breathing, both achieving the same thing.

THE FOUR-FOLD BREATH: First off, we get comfortable with breathing in deeply from our belly area whereupon we start to fill up our lower lungs first, and then as our lungs fill we expand our upper chest area to ensure we fully fill the upper part of our lungs as well. To start with, we can sense it as two parts of our in-breath, and as we get more used to it, we can allow this to be one deep and continuous in-breath.

Secondly, we get comfortable with holding our breath after that deep in-breath, but not forcing or straining our lungs, rather feeling ourselves lifted upwards by our lungs and relaxing into the expansive feeling of the breath within us. Then we get used to starting to release our breath calmly on the out-breath, and allow our lungs to fully empty. As we sense the end of our exhale we relax into the feeling of being completely without breath and relax into this space of no-breath, pausing for a moment before then starting to gradually inhale again from the belly and then from the upper chest, as before.

Now we are comfortable with the flow of in-breath, gentle pause, out-breath, gentle pause, and in-breath again, we can start to bring in a 4-4-4-4 timing. We count internally to ourselves one, two, three, four as we are breathing in, and then count one, two, three, four as we pause holding our breath before the exhale, and then count one, two, three, four while fully exhaling, then as we pause at the end of the out-breath we count one, two, three, four before then starting the inhale again and beginning another round of counting 4-4-4-4.

Let's try and do four or five of these cycles of controlled breathing. As we get more comfortable with this controlled breathing, we can do ten or so rounds, but four or five rounds is enough to start rebalancing the sympathetic and parasympathetic aspects of our autonomic nervous system, in turn helping cohere our three brains and overall bodymind sensory, cognitive and nervous network. Try it out. It costs nothing and yet has immediate benefits on our awareness and outlook, as well as enhancing the connectivity and plasticity of our neural networks, while promoting a general feeling of wellbeing.

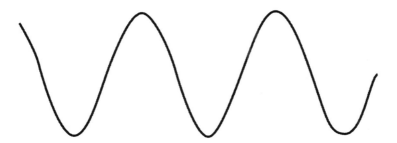

SINE-WAVE BREATHING: Another variation of conscious breathing which is slightly different from the four-fold breath is sine-wave breathing. Here we visualise our breathing in and out as following a coherent sine wave pattern – smooth and evenly regulated crests and troughs of the wave. The movement from the trough rising up to the crest is our in-breath, and the top of the crest being a gradual shift of our in-breath moving into out-breath. Rather than holding the in-breath and out-breath, we are going to be a little gentler in our movement of breath and sense ourselves slowly shifting from the in-breath into the out-breath while pausing a little so we slightly elongate the shift from in to out, and vice versa as we go down the wave from the crest toward the trough with our out-breath, fully exhaling and then slightly pausing before our in-breath as we go through the trough, then starting the in-breath again as we go up the wave cycle once more.

We are going to count to five on the in-breath and likewise on the out-breath. The more relaxed we are the more we may find it easy and natural to elongate the breathing in and breathing out part of the wave (perhaps counting to seven rather than five, or counting slower). Let's say we breathe in through the count of five and then, when our lungs are full, we sense ourselves going over the crest of the wave in our mind-visualization. As we go over the crest we gently move from the end of the in-breath into the beginning of the out-breath, and this can happen over the count of one, two, three. On the number three in our mind we have started the out-breath and then begin the count from one through to five again, just like with the in-breath. When we get to five our lungs are fully empty and we sense ourselves going through the trough of the wave as we go through the count of three again and then start the in-breath on the three, to start us off on our count of one to five again with the next wave.

The slight difference of this practice compared with the four-fold breath technique is that on the count of three, at the crest and trough, we subtly sense the shift from out-breath to in-breath and vice versa rather than purposefully holding no-breath at the end of the out-breath and in-breath cycle like we did in the last exercise. In this sine-wave breathing, it is only on the count of 'two' during our one, two, three crest and trough movement that there is no breath movement at all. It is a more gradual and subtle shift which brings our awareness into the transition between in and out-breath.

The more we practice conscious breathing the more we get used to bringing our consciousness into our breath. Then, the more we can apply this in the busyness of whatever we are doing. Regardless of what we are up to, we are always breathing and so can always be reminded of the inner-sensation of this rhythm. We may start to get used to catching ourselves when we are stressed, irritable, impatient or defensive and so practice a couple of conscious breaths to ourselves while noticing our tension easing. For instance, in the midst of a stressful yet important decision-making meeting we may apply this conscious breathing to enhance our head, heart and gut coherence and so helping us draw on more of our innate generative wisdom sources within us, rather than operating solely from an ego-grasping, left-hemispheric, fire-fighting, reactive, defensive mode.

OPEN AND CLOSED MODES OF MIND

The famous creative John Cleese once gave a talk on creativity to a large business audience which is both witty and well-researched. (Note 14) The essence of the talk is that we all have natural creativity within us, it is part of what makes us alive, and we can learn to cultivate this creativity while enhancing our ability to call upon it in constructive ways at work.

We all exhibit what John Cleese calls 'open mode' and 'closed mode' ways of being (which correspond to McGilchrist's right and left hemispheric ways of attending). The open mode (predominantly right hemisphere) is relaxed, expansive, more inclined to humor, and is curious for its own sake, playful and unbounded. The closed mode (left hemisphere) is action-orientated, anxious, impatient, focused on getting-the-job-done, ticking the to-do list, fire-fighting, reacting rather than being creative, more of a 'doing' imperative than a 'being'.

Cleese notes that most of the time in our working environment, we are in the closed mode and the more we can allow ourselves to bring in our open mode the more creative, innovative and adaptive our work style and team dynamics will be.

To get into the open mode Cleese suggests we need five things: space, time, more time, confidence, and humor. Let's briefly explore these:

We create space in our schedule, taking time out for at least an hour but no more than an hour and a half. We find a quiet space for this specific period of time where we cannot be interrupted or disturbed. An 'oasis-of-quiet' is created by setting boundaries of space and time.

We sit comfortably and start to ponder on the problem at hand. To start with, and perhaps even for the first 15 minutes or so, our ego-chatter will race about in our minds and we will feel the need to get on with pressing matters which we have just remembered need to be done. This is quite natural and we need to sit through this head-noise with dedication yet relaxation. Hence 'more time' is needed as it can take a while for us to start opening up beyond the grasping grip of our ego-mind to allow the 'open mode' (more soulful, intuitive and embodied mode) to start enriching our awareness as our ego-chatter begins to settle down and subside.

We rest against the problem gently in our mind, exploring the problem in a friendly non-urgent way yet in a persistent way, while resisting the urge to go with any immediate 'solutions' that start to crop up. Having a note pad to hand helps as we can jot down some of the things that come into our mind as well as unloading ourselves from the burden of having to remember the errands and things-to-do our racing ego-mind starts to fixate upon.

We may well find it uncomfortable to sit with the problem while solutions start to crop up, and hence why we need confidence in ourselves and this process, because the longer we sit with the problem, the more creative, innovative and original our solutions become. Learning to tolerate this discomfort and mild anxiety of not having a fix to our problem, while resisting the temptation to grab an early solution that crops up, allows us to maximize our pondering time and ensure more insightful solutions emerge. Hence the 'more time' and 'confidence' of Cleese's five things, because it is through embracing more pondering time with confidence in ourselves to stay open, rather than grasping at first-come solutions, that ensures richer creativity. Also, we need confidence to simply play, to explore beyond the usual boundaries of what we might deem sensible, logical or suitable.

This is where humor comes in. Whether we are on our own or with one or two other people, lightening up our mood with humor allows a more expansive open mode to form along with more playfulness in our explorations, as the more outrageous our explorations and the more 'mistakes' we make the better. In fact, in this playful period there are no 'mistakes', anything can be explored, and if we are with other people, we need to ensure we do not judge the others' suggestions or frown or dismiss suggestions as that is a sure way to curtail creativity and playfulness. The more we giggle, laugh and loosen up the better. Then, more novel and insightful solutions will start to emerge after about an hour of this play.

We need to be aware that sometimes solutions will pop up from our unconscious depths at a period of time after the session, perhaps in the shower the next morning, for instance. So we ought to leave some 'cooking' time to allow our deeper unconscious to mull over things and bring up gems from our depths after the event.

Once we have a solution we are happy with, then we need to revert to the closed mode to start to implement it. It is no good still being in the open mode when we are trying to focus on project managing the implementation of the solution.

Yet, we ought to regularly make space in our schedules for such an oasis-of-quiet regardless of whether we feel we need specific creative solutions, as it allows us to nurture this open mode within us, while ensuring a coherence of our left and right brain hemispheres on a regular basis. This enriches our perspective throughout our working week.

REFLECTIVE QUESTIONS

Can you sense periods at work when you get stressed, reactive and defensive to the detriment of what you are trying to solve or work on, and perhaps also to the detriment of others you are working with? On average, how often per week do you feel like this?

When you practice the conscious breathing exercises do you sense a shift in your awareness and mood? How would you describe this subtle shift? Try and think of some descriptions you would apply to this subtle shift in feeling. Could you envisage it helping you de-stress in times of tension?

Are you able to create an oasis-of-quiet in your schedule once a week? Is there anything preventing you from making it happen? Can you work around these preventions if you set your mind to it?

Can you sense what it feels like when your awareness is more in the closed-mode or left-hemispheric orientation (narrowed-down, reductive, focused, and solution-orientated) compared to when your awareness is more in the open-mode or right-hemispheric orientation (expansive, playful, creative, empathic and relational)?

Are there particular activities that you undertake during your week which require more of one mode than the other? Have a go at listing different activities you regularly undertake in a normal week and map these to the two different states. Perhaps some of these activities require an integration of both states simultaneously?

In terms of Barrett's seven stages of psychological development (surviving, relating, differentiating, transformation, internal cohesion, making a difference, and service) which stage resonates most strongly with where you are in your life at the moment?

What can you envisage doing (and being) differently in order to embrace further stages in your psychological development?

What natural passions, strengths, talents and callings do you sense within yourself? List them out and ponder on them for a while. How can you allow these to flow more readily into your work-life?

Are there times during your daily experiences when you can sense the ego-soul dynamic within you? Can you sense when your awareness is more ego-dominated by projections, judgements and thought-chatter or when it is more soulful, expansive, compassionate and insightful?

Reflect on how you might shape your daily routine and weekly schedule differently within the bounds of your obligations to allow for a more coherent ego-soul dynamic to start developing within you and your work-style. What activities or practices could you start to bring into your routine? Are there any practices, exercises or techniques friends or colleagues have mentioned that intrigue you?

Starting my day up open space helps

MODULE **FOUR**

PERSONAL GNOSIS

TRANSFORMING OUR ORGANIZATIONS
AND IMPROVING OUR WORLD STARTS
WITH EACH OF US TAKING PERSONAL
RESPONSIBILITY FOR HOW WE ARE
RELATING WITH REALITY, THE INTENTION
AND ATTENTION WE HOLD, AND THE
WAY IN WHICH WE RELATE WITH, LEAD
AND INSPIRE OTHERS.

EXECUTIVE SUMMARY

- The stresses and strains of our everyday working life take their toll on us, and if we do not adequately renew ourselves, we undermine our potential for greatness.

- There are deep sources of wisdom within and all around us, which we have largely lost access to, so caught-up we have become in our busyness.

- The more we learn to cultivate our natural soulful awareness amidst our everyday busyness, the more we start to call upon more of who we truly are, benefiting our outlook, our relations, our creativity, and our ability to lead in these challenging times.

- As we open up to our soul-calling, we allow our work to become a form of love-in-action, a creative outpouring of our soulful selves in service of life. It is here that our work becomes inherently regenerative.

'GREAT LEADERS ARE AWAKE, AWARE
AND ATTUNED TO THEMSELVES, TO
OTHERS, AND TO THE WORLD AROUND
THEM... [THEY] SEEK TO LIVE IN FULL
CONSCIOUSNESS OF SELF, OTHERS,
NATURE AND SOCIETY.'
RICHARD BOYATZIS AND ANNIE MCKEE,
LEADERSHIP SPECIALISTS

WHETHER WE ARE LEADERS OR team members, entrepreneurs or engineers, this fast-moving world of business, with all its stresses and strains, puts pressure on us. The more able we are to deal with this stress effectively, embracing our challenges as opportunities for deeper learning and growth, the more successful we will be in helping our organizations' journey toward becoming firms of the future. This is about each of us taking personal responsibility for how we engage with life. We can either allow stressful situations to undermine our greatness or we can cultivate a different way of dealing with life, which may well include changing our life situations in radical ways such as changing careers in order to explore what really turns us on.

There is now ample scientific evidence pointing to the detrimental effect stress has on our ability to flourish amid uncertainty. Stress raises our blood pressure, activates hormones (corticosteroids) and inhibits certain brain activity. This impacts the functioning of our immune system, the production of new neurons and the activation of neural circuits (in our brain, heart and gut regions). All of this affects how we relate with ourselves, each other and the world around us. It reduces our creativity, flexibility and capacity to learn. It also makes us feel anxious, agitated, defensive and suspicious. We feel dissonance: a general unease, over-sensitivity, reactive quickness and tendency to interpret situations and other people's actions negatively. This leads to a downward spiral of ineffectiveness, a trail of frustration and antagonism in our wake, unhealthy psychological and physiological reactions, all contributing to further anxiety and dissonance.

Soon we become short-tempered, impatient, frayed-round-the-edges and in need of a drink or two (whether strong coffee or alcohol) to steady ourselves, numb the discomfort or feel temporarily alive again. If we endure long periods in this state, we accentuate and habituate negative thought patterns and emotions, and get caught up in cycles of ego-anxiety and ego-assertiveness while our efficacy and authenticity gets buried. We undermine our personal effectiveness and also undermine the resilience of our organizations. (Note1)

Many of us have experienced bouts of stress and the downward spiraling that ensues. Alas, it is all too common in our organizations these days. And our business context is set to become even more volatile and complex. So what to do?

When we look at the psychological research and leadership development work which has happened over the last few years, we find that it all boils down to taking deliberate and conscious steps within our daily and weekly schedules to cultivate our conscious awareness, to check-in with how we are feeling, to make time and space to refresh and renew our personal presence, awareness and wellbeing. This is about applying tried-and-tested skills and practices that can be folded into our daily work-life in a way that works for us. It's about each of us starting to become masters of our own destiny by cultivating our awareness amid challenging situations; learning, deepening and growing as we go so that each challenging situation can be embraced as an opportunity for us to adapt, enhance, and enrich, rather than setting up downward spirals that undermine us and our organizations.

All the tips and practices throughout this workbook are enjoyable, ease to do and yet deeply enriching if we can find the discipline and dedication to bring them into our schedules. The good news is, this is about each of us opening up to who we really are, peeling back the onion layers of our habituations and acculturations to reveal more of our soulful selves while simultaneously becoming more resilient, effective, courageous and compassionate. As we learn to notice and transcend stress, dysfunction, anxiety and inauthenticity, we make space for the healthier, creative, and convivial aspects of our soulful nature to shine through in us. It is this that makes us better leaders, managers, employees, entrepreneurs, community members, spouses, parents, friends and lovers. In the process, we uncover our soul-calling.

> 'This is the true joy of life, the being used for a purpose recognized by yourself as a mighty one, the being a force of Nature instead of a feverish selfish little clod of ailments and grievances complaining that the world will not devote itself to making you happy.'
> *George Bernard Shaw, writer*

As we have already discussed, this is fundamentally about a shift in consciousness from an ego-dominated awareness toward a more soul-infused awareness; a shift that has been referred to by Jung as individuation, by Maslow and Barrett as self-actualization, and by Wilber as integral consciousness.

Here-on-in, we are going to refer to the cultivation of this more integral, soulful way of being as 'gnosis'. For our Western civilization's founding fathers 'gnosis' meant 'to know', 'to deeply understand', to intimately sense and embody the intuitive, emotional, sensorial and rational aspects of our experience of life. We often overlook the fact that at the foundations of our Western civilization, philosophy and natural science, is a deep understanding of what it means to truly know: a fully embodied soul-infused experience of reality unfettered by the warping perspectives of our dominating ego-awareness.

Gnosis is a dynamic knowing, not a static conceptual state. It is an alive sense of what is continuously emerging in our midst within this very moment, within our inner-worlds and outer-worlds, perceiving both the ephemeral and the eternal aspects of life. It is what some might refer to these days as 'mindfulness' or 'nondual awareness'. Yet, to be clear, this is not a dis-embodied mental state where we negate our lived experience, rather it is an opening up to 'all that is' in our experience of the world through a coherence of our intuitive, rational, emotional and sensorial awareness.

Another ancient Greek word we shall also refer to is 'Sophia'. For the ancients, Sophia meant wisdom, not an intellectualized, theorized version but a fully-lived experience. The ancient Greeks perceived life as innately flowing with the currents of Sophia. To attune ourselves with this wisdom innate within life, is to experience Sophia within us, a wisdom current flowing through the soul, nourishing and enriching our ways of knowing (our gnosis). In developing our gnosis (by cultivating our awareness) we open ourselves up to a more soulful way of attending which is infused (through the soul) with this Sophia, enriching our wise experience of life. Through our coherence of mind (or rather 'bodymind') we allow the deeper wisdom currents of life to flow through our ways of being and doing. (Note 2)

Let's get practical!

First off, we shall explore 'personal gnosis': exploring how we can help cohere our ways of knowing so that we become more effective leaders and team players. Then, in the next module, we will explore 'organizational gnosis': ways in which our organizational practices can enhance our personal and collective gnosis.

When we achieve deep alignment of our ways of knowing within us, we tap into the wisdom of the soul which is an aperture in to the deeper, richer currents of wisdom-grace permeating our inner and outer worlds. When we apply this wisdom through our attention, relations, interactions and work, our work becomes love-in-action, a creative outpouring of our soulful selves in service of life. Through our actions and relations we are allowing this wisdom to enrich what we are doing. Life inevitably throws up all sorts of challenging twists and turns that provoke habitual thoughts, conditioned behaviors and knee-jerk reactions to well up in us. It is up to you and me to take responsibility for how effectively we let go of old ways of reacting while bringing in richer ego-soul awareness to bear on each evolving situation.

Rather than falling into the us-versus-them, short-termist, ego-logic of old, we can allow ourselves to see beyond the superficial into the deeper perspective of the situation, with compassion and wisdom. Here we adapt and develop our 'sensing and responding' capacity with every life situation. Life provides the perfect, yet challenging and sometimes perplexing, learning environment for us to develop our mastery of this 'sensing and responding' capacity.

We start to become more conscious of when we are reacting to situations with old logic and also experiencing what it feels like to sense and response with our more coherent knowing or 'gnosis'. We learn to sense what our heart-head-gut is saying about the situation; we learn to draw on an integrated IQ/EQ/SQ perspective about what is emerging. Through this we develop a deeper inter-relational nature of engaging with life's unfolding context. And so, life offers us the opportunity to continuously practice and polish-up our mastery by learning to apply our 'new way' while learning to let go of our 'old way'. This is easier said than done, and we naturally find it hard to resist falling back on habituated patterns of reactivity to challenging situations. Old habits die hard. Yet, the more we practice letting go of these old ways, the easier it becomes – practice, practice, practice; no one is perfect and we are all learning as we go.

The more we practice, the more we will come to sense a sweet spot of awareness within us, our soul-flow, and we will sense how different this feels to us than the ego-dominant way of attending. The more conscious we become of this subtle shift the more we can learn to encourage it into our awareness. The trick here is not to allow any particular way of knowing (whether emotional intelligence, analytical thinking, or gut reactions, for instance) to be overly dominant. We can help ourselves with this by learning to sense the somatic awareness of our bodies and the subtle felt-sense of our heart-awareness and gut-awareness, so that we can bring this in to counter-act the grasping nature of our head-thinking and its ego-chattering stream of thoughts. By learning to actually feel our gut and heart-awareness, we can more readily tune-in through feeling rather than thinking, which brings our conscious awareness out of our heads.

This can be difficult to do especially in stressful, ever-changing, unpredictable situations that test and push us beyond our comfort zone. In times of uncertainty our ego feels vulnerable. This is a good sign that we are actually pushing ourselves beyond our normal status quo and so adapting to change. But amid this vulnerability, fear will inevitably rise within us and this fear, if left unchecked, can fuel the ego while drowning out our soul-awareness.

All too easily we can grasp for control, analysis, certainty and predictability or judgement, blame and projection amid this fear of uncertainty and sense of vulnerability. It is in the midst of all this that we need to be ever-conscious of what we are feeling and thinking, catching our thoughts, feelings and subtle sensations emerging within us. The more we practice, the more experienced we shall be, and also the more faith we develop in calling upon our different ways of knowing. We begin to trust ourselves to be open and vulnerable to 'what is' rather than grasping at the urge to react, defend or control.

'Vulnerability sounds like truth and feels like courage.'
Brene Brown, researcher and storyteller

This is essentially about us beginning to acquaint ourselves, get familiar with, and gradually fall in love with, our different ways of knowing within ourselves. It is what the ancients meant by the famous phrase 'Know Thy Self'. The Greeks and the Egyptians – the wise ancient founders of Western civilisation – put the words 'Know Thy Self' above the entrance of their most sacred temples. To enter the temple is symbolic of crossing the threshold from ego-awareness to soul-awareness, and for that, the prerequisite is to know thy self. Ancient wisdom traditions the world over recognize how this deep and intimate self-mastery is paramount if we are to attend to life in a wise way. It is this wise way of attending that is the bedrock upon which regenerative business is founded, otherwise we are building on sand and our good intentions along with our well-crafted ethical charters, values-based propositions, sustainability initiatives and mission statements will not stand the test of time.

In a moment we will be diving into a number of easy and enjoyable practices to help us cultivate this personal gnosis.

Before we do so, let's just recap what we have covered here so we are clear on what we mean by personal gnosis, as this forms an important foundation for us: gnosis means 'to know', not in some abstract, theoretical, rationalizing way but to truly know with our whole being, whereupon we directly perceive life as it really is with our true nature. This is a fully embodied experience and when we access this sweet spot of awareness it feels like our inner and outer worlds cohere as we presence the here-and-now of reality in a vivid and vibrant way, with every sinew of our bodies and every cell of our minds alive and present. It can feel like a home-coming as this authentic engagement with reality is something the soul yearns for, and it can also remind us of when we were children, when we were more able to experience life in such an unadulterated and emancipated way, before our attention got twisted and warped by acculturations and habituations.

Peter Reason, in his book *Spindrift*, notes that our lives are often full of tiny, easily overlooked moments when the social constructs of our reality fall away, whereupon we sense more clearly what it is to be human, allowing for a deeper more soulful conversation with the world around us. (Note 3) Our journeying toward gnosis allows us to bring in more of these subtle shifts in awareness into our daily working lives for the benefit of our wellbeing, creative potential and resilience, benefiting our organizations in their journeying toward becoming firms of the future.

> 'The greatest voyage of our lifetimes is not in the seeking
> of new landscapes but in the seeing with new eyes.'
> *Marcel Proust, philosopher*

These brief moments of gnosis offer mini threshold crossings for us. We reach beyond the 'I' perspective of 'old logic', seeing beyond the narrowing-down lens of our ego-awareness, shifting our way of attending with the world. We may find - if only for the briefest of moments to begin with - that we quite naturally and gracefully commune and co-create with others in a coherent, authentic, compassionate and wise way. In this natural state of awareness, we are simply 'being regenerative'. The more we experience this gnosis by opening up our perceptual horizon through developing our ego-soul dynamic, the more practiced we become at allowing this soul-flow to enter into our daily consciousness.

The beauty of this gnosis is that when we open up to 'what is' we also open our bodyminds up to the deeper resonances and rhythms of natural grace within and all around us, the life-force of creation flows unencumbered through us, enriching and rejuvenating us; we find harmony with Nature.

> 'He who is harmony with Nature hits the mark without effort and apprehends the truth without thinking.'
> *Confucius, sage*

This wisdom of Nature is far beyond anything our rationalizing minds can grasp. Yes we can analyze and extrapolate useful insights from the natural world in terms of patterns, process, principles and ecological designs: enter the rapid take-up of biomimicry, nature-inspired design, closed-loop economics, industrial ecology and living-systems thinking, along with the nature-inspired business principles of a firm of the future explored in the previous module. Yet, the Nature we refer to here (with a capitalized N) is both physical and metaphysical, both matter and mind, everywhere. Permeating through everything in our world from the cells in our bodies to our communities and ecosystems runs a wild wisdom quite beyond words. This is what the ancient Greeks sensed as the wisdom of Sophia flowing through Life. This is not just the province of philosopher and poet; it's a natural grace, a very real and potent presence in our daily lives. It is this deeper soulful, Sopheric wisdom we now need to call upon in helping our organizations become truly regenerative.

TIP

OPENING TO NATURE

This activity involves going outside and sitting on the ground for about five minutes or more, so we need to ensure we are dressed appropriately. Let's find a tree that attracts our attention, and sit down next to its trunk, making ourselves comfortable. It is best if we sit up right with our back and spine reasonably straight yet remaining relaxed and comfortable with our hands gently resting in our lap or down by our side, and our legs crossed or stretched out, which ever we prefer. Once we are settled comfortably, we can undertake a few rounds of conscious breathing, feeling the fresh air filling our lungs, and releasing any nagging thoughts through our out-breath. Then, with our eyes closed or slightly open, we simply sit and feel. We don't think, we feel.

Simply feeling our body sensations while we sit is easier said than done as our ego-chattering mind will no doubt try and distract us with discursive thinking. Notice these thoughts and gently and repeatedly bring ourselves back to simply feeling, taking some deep breaths if we feel we need to relax further into this sitting meditation. As we allow ourselves to relax, and our head-chatter starts to wane (which may take a few minutes), let's bring our attention ever-more intensely into the sensations of what we are feeling, whether in our gut, heart, legs, arms or the sensations on our skin, or the noises and gusts of air around us. Then, we can start to bring our awareness into the tree as a living being behind, beneath and above us. Sense the roots radiating out in the soil under us. With our imagination, let's sense the roots spreading into the soil beneath us, deeper and deeper they go. We can then use our imagination to go further into the earth beneath us, all the way into the molten core of our planet, if we wish.

Then, we bring our awareness from deep beneath us back up into the roots of the tree and into our buttocks sitting on the ground next to the tree, and then into our body, up our spine, back and chest, up into our head, and the space above our head. Sense the branches, twigs and leaves radiating and reaching out into the sky above. Sense the clouds and vast expanse above us, taking our awareness up further in to the stars that lie beyond. And then bring our awareness back down into where we are sitting now. Let's just sit here for a couple of minutes with this relaxed awareness of the feelings within us and the world all around us. This is a lovely little practice that we can do once a week or perhaps more frequently if we wish.

> 'When we tie in with the life force it rights us from our distractions and reconnects us to the rapture of life.'
> *Richard Strozzi-Heckler, psychologist*

For our ancient Greek founders of Western philosophy, the term 'philosophy' was not about abstract intellectualized musings but an enlivened embodied experience of life as it really is. The word 'philosophy' came from Pythagoras some five centuries before Christ. Pythagoras married the word 'philia' (meaning 'to embrace, reciprocate and love') with Sophia (the goddess of wisdom) to make the word 'philosophy'. The ultimate goal of philosophy for our ancient forebearers was to learn to attune our ways of knowing with the wisdom of Sophia innate within Nature.

At the springs of all great civilizations, and the ancient shamanic and tantric traditions of indigenous cultures the world over, we find this perennial philosophy. This ancient yet timeless wisdom has largely been lost amid today's corporate and consumerist obsession with the pursuit of short-term material betterment. All-too-consumed we have become with ego-gratification, we choke the soul severing ourselves from our source of wisdom, cutting ourselves off from any deep and lasting happiness, ruining our planet in the process. To refer to Einstein's insights, when we honor our servant to the extent of forgetting our sacred gift we entrap ourselves in a devastating delusion.

> 'And now here is my secret, a very simple secret, it is only with the heart that one can see rightly; what is essential is invisible to the eye.'
> *Antoine de Saint-Exupéry, writer*

HEART AWARENESS

Central to our gnosis is cultivating 'heart-awareness'. What is often overlooked in our biological understanding of the heart is that it is an organ of perception. Recent studies point to it being the body's most powerful electromagnetic sensor and transmitter, continually decoding the vast array of electromagnetic and quantum signals radiating in our lived-in environment. The heart governs our bodymind's sensory, neural, nervous and instinctual systems; 65% of the cells in the heart are neural cells which are wired into the nervous system, gut and brain. (Note 4)

While much of this continual and participatory dialogue with the world around us happens beyond the perceptual horizon of our daily waking awareness, as we develop 'heart-awareness' we can allow ourselves to become more conscious of this wise way of knowing. And with this comes a richer sense of perceiving subtle fluctuations in our bodymind's capacity for knowing - our 'somatic awareness'. Developing heart-awareness, therefore, enriches our intuitive mind and also enriches our embodied ways of sensing and responding with the world around and within us.

'Unlike the egoic operating system, the heart does not perceive
through differentiation. It doesn't divide the field into inside
and outside, subject and object. Rather, it perceives by means
of harmony…When heart-awareness becomes fully formed
within a person, he or she will be operating out of nondual
consciousness…where they will discover the resources they
need to live in fearlessness, coherence, and compassion – or in
other words, as true human beings.'
Cynthia Bourgeault, contemplative and priest. (Note 5)

Studies prove that becoming more conscious of our heart-
awareness has healing effects on our bodymind: invoking
feelings of love through our hearts can shift us from a state of
dis-ease toward wellbeing, with hormonal changes and
beneficial alterations in our brain-wave frequencies, along with
increased rates of tissue repair and stem-cell and neuron
production. As we become more practiced at developing heart-
awareness, we can develop what is called 'heart entrainment',
where our brain-wave patterns form a coherence across our left
and right brain hemispheres and also start to entrain with the
deeper wave-vibrations of our heart and gut regions. With this
come the immediate benefits of heightened mental clarity,
improved decision making, increased responsiveness and
resiliency to change, efficiency of energy use, increased creativity
and innovation, along with improved emotions of general
happiness, empathy, compassion and conviviality – all important
contributors in shifting our organizations toward regenerative,
purposeful firms of the future!

Here are three techniques for cultivating heart-awareness, each
practice builds upon the other, and we can call upon aspects of
each of these as we go about our business. They require no credit
card only our quality of intention and attention; they are: 1) heart
breathing 2) heart entrainment 3) head-heart-gut coherence: (Note 6)

TIP

HEART BREATHING

Whether you are sitting or standing, first off become aware of your breath. As you breathe in and out, feel your lungs move up and down and your stomach in and out. Feel the breath in your nostrils, cool as it comes in, warm as it goes out. Let's embark on a couple of rounds of conscious breathing to settle our awareness and bring our attention into our bodies while allowing grasping thoughts to ease as our awareness deepens. If the situation allows, we can place both hands over our heart area, one hand above the other, so one is covering the lower heart region and the other the upper heart region of our chest area in a gentle way. If the situation does not allow, then we can simply imagine we are placing our hands over our heart area and bring our attention into our heart region as we do so.

Then, with our imagination, we breathe in and out through the heart area (as if breathing through where our hands are placed over our heart). Do a few rounds of this heart breathing, breathing in and out deeply and consciously as we focus on the heart area. This 'heart breathing' amplifies our heart-awareness while helping our bodymind coherence within us (improving our sympathetic and parasympathetic network alignment as well as our left and right brain coherence). We may notice a subtle shift in how we feel, perceive and attend to what is emerging around us; a simple yet profound shift in consciousness from head to heart occurs within us no matter how fleeting.

TIP

HEART ENTRAINMENT

Let's find a space where we can be free to relax uninterrupted for four minutes - this could well be the office toilet or nearby park bench, for instance, unless our organization happens to have dedicated quite spaces which, alas, is still the exception rather than the rule, but times they are a changing! When comfortable, we start with the practice of heart breathing, as before.

Then, when we feel ourselves breathing deeply and calmly in and out through our heart region, we use our imagination to recall a memory and feeling of something we really love (this might be, for instance, a memory of a pet we have or once had, a favourite song, a walk in nature, playing with our children, a special memory of a time in our lives when we felt really happy and alive – it does not matter what it is, only that it invokes a feeling of love within us). While still doing our heart breathing, we conjure up this feeling of love, and re-live this loving feeling with our imagination, really feeling it in our heart. Then, we allow this loving feeling to start to expand from our heart region throughout our body. Feel this loving feeling spread into our legs and arms, our toes, fingers and spine, our neck and head, all over our body; allow ourselves to indulge in this feeling, immerse ourselves in it, as we continue with our heart breathing. Feel every cell and sinew in our body being washed and cleansed with this feeling of love.

As we allow ourselves to relax into this feeling of love, we undertake an affirmation, which we can either verbalize softly out loud, or if the situation dictates we can simply say it in our mind: 'I am able to fully love myself'. Repeat this statement over and over at least five times to ourselves while we are still heart breathing and still feeling this expanded feeling of love. Then, we simply relax and sit for a few moments, for as long as our situation allows us. Again, notice how our perception, awareness and way of attending to 'what is' in our lives at this moment has subtly shifted compared to how we were before we undertook the exercise.

As we practice this exercise more and more, we can change our affirmation to be something related to an improvement we would like to see occur in our relations with our work environment. As long as the affirmation has a loving intent (for example, 'I am able to lovingly accept my boss for who she is', or 'I am able to compassionately listen and empathize with my team members') it will help reprogram patterns of behavior within us, allowing us to cultivate heart-awareness within ourselves while alleviating our ego-reactions to situations.

'The best and most beautiful things in the world cannot be seen nor touched but are felt in the heart'.
Helen Keller, political activist

TIP

HEAD-HEART-GUT COHERENCE

Like with the heart entrainment exercise, we find a space where we can be free to relax uninterrupted for at least four minutes. We start with the heart breathing and then move on to the heart entrainment exercise, as above. Then, rather than doing the affirmation, we consciously bring our feeling of love into our head and notice what thoughts arise; we notice these thoughts without getting overly involved in them while being conscious of maintaining our loving feeling. It is quite normal for judgemental or anxious thoughts to creep in, and as this happens we simply notice them and cultivate the feeling of love again while bringing our attention to our heart breathing. Bringing our awareness back to our heart breathing provides a great anchor.

As we move our conscious awareness from the head back down into the heart region, we remain in the heart for a few breaths and sense what it feels like, and then we move this awareness down into our gut region and sense what it feels like to be in the gut region (our navel area and abdomen), noticing any emotions, feelings, thoughts, sensations – but resisting the temptation to judge or form opinions about these subtle sensations, we just sit with the sensations. It is normal to sense fear or anxiety, yet we try not to react to these feelings or suppress them, but simply let them be. We use our heart breathing to bring ourselves back to the feeling of love if we are starting to get caught up in other emotions. We then move our attention, and feeling of love, from our gut back into our heart region and allow it to just remain there for a while and notice any subtle differences in feelings and felt-sensations. This particular activity can be a useful one to undertake at the end of a stressful day, perhaps just after some light stretching exercises such as T'ai chi or Qi Gong movements.

✎

The more we allow ourselves to feel this awareness of our subtle body sensations, the more we are cultivating our heart-awareness and also our overall body (or 'somatic') awareness, learning to sense what it feels like to be in our head, heart or guts. This not only allows us to free ourselves from the ego-chattering ruminations of our thinking head, but also to start to release old tensions, habituations, psychic wounds, projections and held-beliefs that have become suppressed within unconscious 'shadow' aspects of our psyche and encoded in our bodymind. By cultivating this awareness we can allow aspects of our shadow to emerge into the light of our waking consciousness and so begin to integrate more of our psyche. This helps our intuitive, emotional, somatic and rational awareness to blend, alchemize and cohere into an enriching gnosis, helping us become wiser in our receptivity and responsiveness to life situations.

BODY AWARENESS

What is often referred to as 'somatic awareness' is fast being recognized as an important tool for leadership and organizational development. Somatic awareness is about learning to bring our attention out of our heads and into our bodies. (Note 7)

Our soma is our body, or as the scientist Candice Pert would say, our bodymind, including all its natural ways of knowing. By re-orientating our awareness away from our incessant ego-chattering discursive mind into our body sensations we develop a more embodied experience of mind integrated into body.

The more we learn to listen to our soma, the better we are at developing our inner-sense by feeling the subtle sensations of our body – tingles in the hands, cool air movement around our nostrils, throat constrictions, eye movements, heart pangs, gut reactions, and such like. Rather than noticing and reacting upon or suppressing these feelings, we open up our attention to them. We simply bring our conscious awareness into these sensations. By allowing our awareness to go into the arising experiences within our body, we enter a way of knowing that is pre-judgement, freed from the discursive conceptualizations of our thinking mind. With this, we find a spaciousness opening up within us, a distancing from our ego-chatter, a softening and deepening of our awareness.

As we learn to bring our awareness into our bodily sensations, we can start to touch reality as it is, experienced by us prior to judgement, reaction and apprehension. We start to re-member the continuous flow of energy within us and the deeper array of experiences which lie within us all the time, yet much of the time unnoticed or suppressed by our busy thinking mind. This awareness helps us to experience a more embodied sense of our being-in-the-world, our poiesis: a continual communing with our world through these felt-senses, intuitive insights and emotional sensations.

Studies now show us that our hearts, guts and bodymind networks sense and respond with our environments in a variety of ways (sensorial, electromagnetic, quantum) triggering felt-senses, constrictions, tensions, energy releases and a variety of sensations which, as we become more conversant with them, can enhance our ability to make wise complex relational decisions quickly.

It takes time and practice to develop deep somatic awareness, in part because we have become culturally anesthetized; our systems of education have prioritized the rational-analytical thinking head to such an extent that it's a cultural-norm to ignore or suppress our somatic awareness. As business coach, Julio Olalla, insightfully notes, 'The dominant epistemology of our times fundamentally reduces learning and knowing to exercises of a disembodied intellect. This way of knowing is at the heart of the huge crises humanity is facing right now. A deep and lasting transformational learning requires in each of us a shift in the dynamic coherence of our linguistic, emotional and somatic being.'

Through simple practices such as breathing into parts of our body and holding our attention there in a receptive way, we can start to develop intimacy with our somas.

TIP

SOMATIC EXPLORATION

Let's find a quiet space where we will not be disturbed for ten minutes and can feel safe and comfortable enough to lie on the floor. We need to make sure we are warm enough; perhaps placing a rug over us as we lie down because the body cools down as it relaxes during this practice.

Now, let's simply lie down, get comfortable and relax.

Feel the weight of our body on the floor as we lie here, feel our breathing in and out of our lungs as we undertake a couple of rounds of conscious breathing.

We are now going to do a quick 'body scan' which we do by scanning our awareness over our bodies, moving our attention from our toes up our legs, hips, up the back and chest, each arm and then neck and head. Then, while breathing deeply, we sense into any tensions, pains or sensations in our body and allow our awareness to go into those places in our body. We are not trying to force or control or manage anything, we simply allow our awareness to notice a tension or sensation and see what emerges. Perhaps the sensation may change slightly or memories may be invoked in our mind or the sensation may remind us of something. We can play with this practice for a while, bringing our awareness back to the sensation each time it drifts off.

When we feel ready, we can scan our body from toes to head again and sense into another area of our body, perhaps our back or neck or a place that is feeling tight or tense; once again, simply let our awareness go into that feeling for a few moments. We inquiry gently into the sensation and see what comes. This is a relaxing and easy way to start relating with our body sensations.

At this point, we can either get up slowly and gently to end the practice, or, if we have the time and space available, we can stay lying down and start to engage in some contemplative questions with ourselves and sense the body sensations that may arise upon us asking these questions while attending to our body. Here are a couple of questions we might wish to ask ourselves while sensing into how our bodies feel as we ponder each question in our mind in an open, non-judgemental way for a few moments. A first question might be, 'How do I experience the feeling of loving myself?' We gently ask that question over and over a couple of times in our mind and then scan our body and sense what it feels like for the body to respond to the question. We might sense subtle shifts, tensions or sensations in certain areas, if so, let's go into those areas and just explore while gently holding the question in mind.

After a few moments, we might ask the question, 'How do I experience love for others?' And again we feel into the body, asking our body the question, sensing any subtle sensations. Then we could ask, 'How do I experience freedom?' And again we feel into the body, asking the question and sense. We are mindful of when our attention wanders off into discursive thoughts, memories or stories, gently bringing our attention back into our body sensations.

Next we can ask, 'How do I experience happiness?' And again we feel into the body while asking our body the question. And finally, 'What is my sense of purpose, my soul-calling?' And again we feel the sensations, going into the sensations for a few moments, just being with the sensations in our body in a relaxed receptive way. There are no right or wrong sensations or feelings, whatever we experience is right for that moment. When we are ready, we can finish off with a couple of rounds of conscious breathing before sitting up slowly and gently.

TIP

CONSCIOUS WALKING

This activity is best done outside with bare feet, but it can also be done inside with shoes on, say in a corridor or long room with plenty of space ahead of us. Firstly, we stand still. We feel our body just standing upright, on the spot. We feel the sensations, our hands, our feet, the weight of our body on the soles of our feet. We breathe consciously and deeply a couple of times and do a quick body scan with our attention, starting from the feet and going through all of our body to the top of our head.

With intimate awareness of our body, we gradually lift one leg up as if taking a step but in slow motion, becoming conscious of how the leg feels as we lift it up, sensing the weight going on the other leg as we maintain balance, sensing our leg stretching out and then the feeling of slowly placing it down again as we step forward. Feel the rest of our body moving forward and our weight shifting as we maintaining balance.

Next, we take another slow step with the other leg, again feeling the body sensations, the balance and weight distribution, our back posture and our arms moving slightly. We take a couple more slow steps maintaining our awareness in the body, noticing our balance and felt-sensations. And then we start to quicken the speed of the steps just a little bit with each step, until we are beginning to walk faster than we usually would, still feeling the body movements and sensations keenly within us. Then, we start to slow the strides down gradually, slower and slower; feel the balancing, the weight shifting. Eventually we are so slow in our steps that our movement is very gradual, as slow as we can go without losing balance. Then we stop. We scan our whole body again with our awareness as we stand still on the spot, noticing any sensations.

We then go about our normal business while being mindful of the conscious feeling of our strides as we walk. In this way, the everyday act of walking becomes a practice for cultivating somatic awareness and mindfulness.

TIP

YOGA NIDRA

This is an ancient practice of full-body deep relaxation that cultivates a state of consciousness between being awake and asleep, a state where we become increasingly aware of our inner body awareness. It can help promote healthy sleeping, enhance our general wellbeing, and helps us tame our ego, all while gaining access to deeper wisdom.

First, we find a warm and comfortable space where we are able to lie down undisturbed for at least fifteen minutes. This exercise can be done in bed, and as it helps promote sleeping, it can be practiced just before going to sleep, but also during the day too, as a way of helping get ourselves into a creative more soulful space (John Cleese's 'open mode') rather than sending us to sleep.

We lie down on the ground with a rug over us, or in bed, and we settle ourselves comfortably. Feel the weight of our body resting on the floor or bed beneath. Feel the sensation of our clothes against our skin, and feel our lungs rising up and down as we breathe. Bring our awareness to our breathing, notice our lungs filling and emptying, and take a couple of deep breaths in and out, and feel the body starting to relax. Notice any tensions and sensations, becoming intimately aware of how the body is feeling overall. We then scan through the body from toe to head swiftly with our awareness. We can take a couple more deep breaths and then bring our attention into our left foot, with specific focus. Let's really feel the left foot with our awareness, feel the sensations. We imagine what it's like to be inside our left foot.

Now we are going to move through our different body parts with our awareness, starting with the big toe on our left foot, then moving to each individual toe, then to the sole of the foot, the arch and then the ankle. We move our attention to our shin on our left leg, then to the back calf, up to the front of the knee, and the back of the knee, up our thigh to our left hip, and then up the left side of our body to our armpit. Next, we sense our left shoulder, our biceps, then triceps, our elbow and then our left forearm, wrist, palm, back of the hand, thumb, first finger, second finger, third finger, fourth finger, and fifth finger.

Now, we bring our attention to our right foot and start with the big toe and move along the toes, the sole, arch and ankle, up the leg, thigh, hip, side, armpit, arm, hand and fingers as per the left side, ensuring we touch each part with our conscious awareness catching ourselves when we drift off, always bringing our attention back to the body.

When we have finished the right side, ending with the right fingers, we then bring our awareness into the base of our spine and our buttocks, and then we move our awareness all the way up the spine, sensing all over our back as we move up the spine, up to the neck. Then we focus on the neck, back of the head, top of the head, forehead, left eye-brow, right eye-brow, nose, tip of the nose, left cheek, right cheek, left ear, right ear, lips, tongue, chin, throat, collar bone, left side of the chest, right side of the chest, diaphragm, feel it moving up and down with our breathing. We bring awareness to our heart area, to our stomach, to the organs in our stomach region, then lower abdomen, down to our sex glands and base of the spine.

Then we feel our whole body, we feel its aliveness as we breathe into every part of our body. We do a quick body scan to feel all around the body, notice the subtle energy flowing freely, and feel every part of our body alive with this energy; then we take a few deep breaths and simply relax into this feeling for as long as time allows us.

It is quite normal to fall asleep while doing this exercise, and if our schedule allows, that's fine as it is rejuvenating. The more we practice it, the more proficient we will become at remaining in a conscious yet deeply relaxed, spacious state without falling asleep. This stimulates changes in our brain wave patterns and also our entire bodymind vibrations so that general coherence, greater intuition and wiser soulful awareness are cultivated. It's a powerful practice to get used to, and has profound benefits for us while costing nothing.

This might all feel rather 'New Age' or 'soft and fluffy' for us busy business people to bother with. After all, we have a job to get on with and the challenges are mounting all around us.

Yet, the reality we are faced with is that these increasingly challenging times demand leaders, managers, change agents, decision makers, team members and stakeholders who are able to deal with systemic challenges in authentic and wise ways amid stressful, unpredictable environments. Time and again, leadership and business transformation studies point to the necessity for leaders who are deeply connected, aligned and coherent within themselves. Embodied, somatic awareness is now increasingly recognized across the fields of psychology, leadership and sociology as an important part of aligning our IQ, EQ and SQ, helping us be resilient and effective in our organizations. While it may seem more 'normal' or socially acceptable to embrace yet another 'cook-book' management methodology, what our organizations and wider stakeholder communities desperately need now is for each of us to start taking personal responsibility for cultivating our own gnosis so that we bring in more authenticity, creativity, connection and wisdom into what we do and the way we do it.

> 'We now live in a global economy characterized by rapid change, accelerating scientific breakthroughs and an unprecedented level of competitiveness. These developments create new demands on our psychological resources. Specifically they require a greater capacity for self-management, personal responsibility and self-direction.'
> *Nathaniel Branden, psychotherapist*

Experiential practices are powerful due to what they evoke in us, hence the importance of well facilitated workshops and interventions, and clearly there is only so much a workbook can convey here. With that caveat, here is a mini-exploration aimed at helping convey the different dynamics we are learning to become more conscious of cultivating in our everyday work-life as we develop our gnosis: **receptivity** (an opening up to what is arising within and all around us; a tuning-in to, or sensing into, what is emerging both within and beyond ourselves); **responsiveness** (cultivating our ability to sense and respond authentically to what we are being receptive to); **reciprocity** (the way we inter-relate with others and our world through our responsiveness).

RECEPTIVITY

The degree to which our soulful awareness permeates our daily awareness depends on how receptive we are to what is emerging in the here-and-now. Are we closed-off, caught up in our thinking heads, stressed-out in our egos? Or are we able to allow our daily awareness to become more spacious, soulful and receptive to what we are sensing through our felt-senses, gut reactions, intuitions, emotions, non-verbal communication signals, and so forth?

The trick here is not to get caught up in thoughts of self-improvement, or attempting to force our awareness to be more receptive. Receptivity comes about through a lightness, a relief and release, an opening up and letting-go, so that we can simply 'be' in this moment, attentive to what 'is' without trying to analyze; just feeling, perceiving, being, without thought-judgements. By simply opening our awareness up to the here-and-now we provide an invitation for our awareness to transcend the self-imaging, self-justifying ego, even if for the briefest of moments.

We may notice our body starting to relax and our breathing deepen, muscular tensions releasing and our senses enlivening. We become simultaneously more relaxed yet more alive and our perspective less acute yet more vivid. Spaciousness starts to appear in our consciousness; less grasping hurriedness, more calm alertness. However, the ego's grasping tendency may not give way to such receptive soulfulness easily, hence practice and commitment is required. There are tried-and-tested techniques to help develop this receptivity such as Vipassana, Yoga Nidra, and Transcendental Meditation, and in the pages ahead, some easy to practice techniques suitable for the busy business environment are offered.

'Meditation is the tool for stepping away from the ego. It is returning to the ground of being from which existence springs. It is the wave remembering that it is not different from the ocean.'
Rashid Maxwell, author

The good news is that cultivating this receptivity is a returning to our natural awareness; it is a remembering of who we truly are; a beginning of walking the path of knowing thy self, a path that once found becomes the only path worth taking. The more we practice and develop this, the more our capacity and ability to tap into it grows. We learn to sense how it feels within us when we tap into this authentic, soulful connection. The more we cultivate this awareness, the more we learn to trust its wisdom, in turn the more we become fearless within the moment and courageous in our response.

TIP

MINDFUL PRACTICE

Here is a simple exercise in becoming mindful of how we are experiencing reality. We ask colleagues, team members or workshop participants to get into pairs. When in our pairs, we are going to share in a non-judgemental way 'what' we are attending to within the moment. For the first three minutes we are going to share back and forth with our partner what is instantly coming up for us, starting each sentence with 'Now I am aware of...' So, we simply share what we are aware of in that moment, with no long pauses between sharing so that it is spontaneous without us overly thinking about what we are going to say. One person shares one sentence, and then the other shares one sentence, going back and forth until the three minutes are up.

Then, during the next three minutes we are going to share in our pairs starting each sentence with 'What I am NOT aware of is...' We instantaneously recall situations, thoughts, sensations, people, places, and such like, that we were not immediately noticing but are now residing on the edge of our awareness, on the fringe of our consciousness. Again, we do not leave long pauses between our sharing so we are spontaneous while recalling things on the periphery of our awareness.

Finally, for the next three minutes, we share starting each sentence with 'I choose to be aware of...' sharing what we choose to be aware of in this moment, again with no long pauses as we take it in turns, back and forth in our pairs sharing a sentence at a time.

This simple yet revealing exercise gives us first-hand experience of the conscious choice we have over what we are attending to and how we are able to transform our stream of thinking. If the pairs are part of a larger team or workshop group, the pairs may wish to feedback to the group as a whole their findings, feelings and learnings. (Note 8)

RESPONSIVENESS

Our responsiveness is our ability to sense and then respond to 'what is' in a soul-infused way. As we allow for our receptivity to deepen with practice and trust, our ability to relate authentically, empathically and creatively with others heightens. Receptivity provides the foundation for our heightened responsiveness.

While contemplative practices such as meditation and yoga help develop our receptivity, we need to be able to sustain this receptive-responsiveness amid our busy work schedules. Finding the right level of receptive-responsiveness for the situation we are in requires continual attunement of our ways of knowing: sensing with our guts and hearts, cognizing with our heads. Some situations may require a more rational, analytical and definitive response while others a more heart-felt empathic listening and sharing, for instance.

A useful metaphor here is of learning to swim (or ride a bike). As we gain confidence in our ability to swim, we allow ourselves to let go of the side for longer and longer periods, freeing ourselves to immerse fully, unimpaired in the art of swimming. It is not easy to let go of old ways so deeply conditioned in our conscious and unconscious psyche and it requires courage and determination. If at first we don't succeed, try and try again. Soon, like riding a bike or swimming, we become proficient enough in the 'new way' that it starts to become instinctual and our ego-awareness with its anxiety eases its incessant control-based reactions and routines. Our way of attending becomes less encumbered by our 'old way' and our creative potential flows freer. We then begin to deeply sense the co-creative, unfolding and emergent venture of life. Yes, it is useful to have plans and clear ideas of where we are going and what we are doing, yet this also needs to be balanced with an openness and adaptability to what emerges. This is the art of living, and what Chris Nichols, professor at Ashridge Business School, calls 'artful knowing'. Through this artful undertaking, our work becomes a conduit for a more soul-infused, purposeful on-going inquiry; an adventure of becoming who we were born to be.

RECIPROCITY

Reciprocity is the way we inter-relate with our ever-changing environment. Upon being responsive to what is emerging, we then engage in relationship with the situation empathically and authentically, in a fully-embodied coherent way, allowing a reciprocating dynamic to unfold. All living systems, including human ones, thrive through reciprocity. Reciprocity is the life-blood that nourishes us; whether it's the small interactions of a wink, smile and supporting comment, or a warm 'hello' and 'thank you', or detailed constructive feedback after a demanding project, each interrelation can be undertaken with varying degrees of heartfelt integrity or cold, judgemental egotistic aloofness or defensiveness. The 'way' we inter-relate affects the paths that open up or close down from that interrelation.

As the former CEO of Hanover Insurance Bill O'Brien noted, 'the success of the intervention depends upon the interior state of the intervener'. How open, authentic and heart-felt we are with our reciprocity will determine the level of flow we experience, and vice versa. The more we are in our soul-flow the more our interrelations will be undertaken in a synchronistic soulful way, and the more we will reap the benefits of what we sow. Yes, there will always be the really difficult situations that seem to be undermining us or pushing our buttons, where our ego is in heightened alert to defend 'self' against 'other' – again this is a useful learning experience in which to practice our gnosis, remaining true to our deeper ways of knowing, sensing and responding without reacting over-defensively or from our base emotions of anger, jealousy, fear or resentment.

If we start to try and control or dominate the flow of exchange during a conversation or emerging situation, we will impede the flow and undermine the greatness of what could have been possible. Aligning our pulses and rhythms with the emerging field of our teams and stakeholders is the artful adventure of life. We learn as we go and mistakes are inevitable, providing us the opportunities to learn and improve.

TIP

THE CO-CREATIVE DANCE OF LIFE

A powerful yet simple illustration of how to bring this receptive-responsive-reciprocating improvisational dance of life consciously alive within us is to learn to dance with one another in a receptive, responsive, reciprocating way. To begin with, two people pair up as partners, a short distance apart with legs astride and touching hands. One of us chooses to be assertive 'leader' and the other yielding 'follower'. At first with a rocking to and fro linear motion, then perhaps transforming into a circular motion, the two of us move together. A rhythm develops, as with a swinging pendulum, but the movement is dependent on the leader's self-centred awareness and associated effort, regardless of what the follower may be experiencing. So the movement could not really be called a 'dance' in the fullest sense, in which each is equally and vitally involved in partnership. The follower might as well not be there: if the leader is tired, the movement will be tired; if the leader is full of energy, the movement will be energetic, but creatively restricted and fatiguing. If at some stage, however, the leader becomes sensitive to the movement of the follower and attunes to this so as to 'follow the follower', the result is a mutual effortlessness where each is alive within the influence of the other. Both of us co-create without a pre-defined trajectory and so improvise in a continually innovative way.

To flow in such an open, mutually inclusive way requires an attuning of our bodymind awareness both to each other and to the co-evolving movement. Correspondingly, the dance itself responds to our ever changing receptive-responsive dynamic. If, for example, while we are dancing co-creatively – with neither trying to lead and both following the communing flow - one partner becomes more assertive, the other may respond either by becoming more yielding or by becoming more resistive. The dance either loses its co-creative fluidity or it becomes tense and jerky. By the same token, if both partners remain passive, the dance won't happen at all. Here, we can sense how reciprocity emerges from a depth of receptive-responsiveness within each partner, and yet the reciprocity emerges beyond either of the two partners, within the dance itself, a synergistic dynamic which both of us flow within. (Note 9)

Another simple yet powerful way of illustrating co-creative reciprocity in groups is when people have to co-create something without talking to each other. Something we tried once, at Schumacher College with a group of workshop participants, was to gather people into groups of five and ask them to open their arms and hands out so their fingers are all touching in a circle.

Then a heavy lump of clay is placed in the middle of the circle of hands of each group, so everyone in each group is co-participating in holding the clay together. Then they are requested to begin moulding the block of fresh clay together in silence, while having to also stand up and hold the heavy block between them. As improvisational moulding unfolds, each participant adds their own creativity without explicitly knowing what the others have in mind. There is no over-arching plan or pre-defined destination, and yet the participants have fun creating a group exhibit they are proud of due to a shared sense of inclusive involvement and team work. A bonding amongst the group forms without words being spoken.

Ultimately, life is a dance of co-creativity. It is a dance that allows us to play with its inherent relational dynamics - receptivity, responsiveness and reciprocity - while attuning our natural ways of knowing. The more receptive, responsive and reciprocating we are able to be, the more engaged with – yet more exposed to – our changing landscape we are. With practice we learn to attune with what works best for our life situations and we learn to open up and tune-in to the creative energies, collective intelligence, wisdom and grace swirling around and within us all the time. Opening up in this way of 'being and doing' requires courage, determination, faith and humility. It is a life-dynamic where we are continuously learning to be true to ourselves, peeling back our onion layers as we open up to more of ourselves through vulnerability and courage.

Gestalt psychologist Dr. Malcolm Parlett, explores this continuous learning and opening up within ourselves and our relations in his book *Future Sense*. He explains how we all need to start cultivating 'whole intelligence' in order to stay sane while living within a world in crisis. By cultivating this 'whole intelligence' (referred to as 'whi' for short) we enable ourselves to be sensitive to present situations while open, adaptive, courageous and resilient enough to deal with the dynamics of the increasingly complex situations facing us. For Parlett, this 'whi' is for everyone regardless of age, education, culture or upbringing, and is not confined to the intellectually gifted.

The more we are conscious of our own awareness, our authenticity and insights, and our reactions and responses, the more we learn to sense what 'feels right or not right' by attuning our bodymind antennae as we go about our daily activities. He notes that, 'humanity urgently needs to discover and refine new ways to stimulate, encourage and expand the range of whole intelligence and the conditions that support its development.' This whi is something that has to be lived, observed, cultivated and explored within our everyday living, and relates with what we have been referring to as 'gnosis' lived through the receptive-responsive-reciprocating life-dynamic we just explored. It is worth us looking at Parlett's five explorations or personal contemplations, as each of these can be undertake within our daily lives to help us cultivate whi: responding; inter-relating; embodying; self-recognizing; experimenting. (Note 10)

RESPONDING

This is an ongoing exploration into the way in which we respond to situations and accomplish outcomes: our capacity to stand back from impulsive reactions, resisting the temptation to jump in too quickly with knee-jerk responds, by pausing and gaining a wider contextual perspective which reads the situation and senses the inter-relational dynamics emerging; situational-reading in the moment while also focusing in on aspects that require immediate attention or further clarification; then having the courage and persistence to respond with authentic leadership by carrying out the required steps with flexibility and adjustment; listening to others as we go and tuning-in to what works and what doesn't; letting go of pre-defined outcomes, cultural biases or personal perspectives while adapting to the transforming context; drawing on implicit and tacit knowledge as well as intuitive hunches and gut reactions while sensing into the collective intelligence of the group; seeking insight from local and regional experts; sharing responsibility and empowering others while facilitating the transformation of tensions into creative insights and constructive ways ahead.

INTER-RELATING

The closer we look, the more we may realize that our world is a rich milieu of inter-relations. Our sense of self is actually defined through these inter-relations and the ways in which we respond to and relate with others: the self becomes 'self' through its relations with others. In our slowing down, sensing into what is emerging, while inquiring and listening, we may notice irritations, tensions, rising emotions in ourselves and in others. The more we tune-in to an unfolding inter-relation with another, the more we can embrace the co-creative dance this relation allows for as we co-participate in 'reading' each other and responding accordingly, while being aware of our own prejudices, judgements and reactions. Our individual awareness also permeates with the collective field of the dance and wider contextual field.

And so this 'inter-relating' is an on-going exploration into: learning to appreciate our creative impulses in the company of others while managing our potential for destructiveness; noticing when we are getting distracted, unsettled, drained, tense or ungrounded, and also noticing any misunderstandings; providing space for dialogue to emerge rather than reactionary argument; allowing ourselves and others to step beyond the 'us and them' separateness of our individualistic tendencies and allowing our conversations and meetings to be more flowing, emergent, creative and open.

Individuality is valued for the differences and diversity of perspectives it brings while also recognizing the need for global frames, an over-arching organizational sense of purpose and inclusive values-based cultural narratives that do not seek to normalize diversity yet provide a unifying ground within which the diversity is rooted.

EMBODYING

This is an exploration into becoming more embodied by: being more conscious of our felt-senses, feelings, emotional states, moods, and feelings of consonance or dissonance with what is unfolding; intimately feeling our human experience of this life through our energetic bodyminds immersed within nested fields of human, more-than-human and quantum spheres; realizing the deep, profound and full ranging extent of our interdependence as individuals, teams, organizations, social networks and more-that-human networks within the matrix of Life; noticing triggers to stress reactions, sensing what contributes to our becoming ungrounded and what contributes to our dancing with grace and love; noticing our gestures and other peoples gestures and body movements and non-verbal signals; re-embodying from our thinking-mind by sensing our breathing and regularly immersing ourselves in the felt-senses of our body; learning to attune with our environment and feel the life-force or 'chi' flowing within us and within everything; becoming aware of the multitude of feedback loops, interconnections, experiences, neural network triggers and subtle perturbations going on within and all around us all the time; enhancing our sensitivity to our surroundings by becoming more conscious of our 'being in the world'.

SELF-RECOGNIZING

The core motive here is cultivating wisdom through our ability to listen and learn from our own insights and interactions with others. This is developed through the on-going exploration of: attending to what is going on within us while integrating views, perspectives, judgements of others and feedback from our wider context; awakening to our natural coherence and clarity within us and also our destabilizing tendencies toward stress, fragmentation, distraction, busyness, gossip and superficial social media; recognizing the constantly changing nature of ourselves and how daily situations help reveal more about ourselves; sensing into the rootedness and rightness of our underlying purpose and core value-set (as Parlett eloquently notes 'boats in strong currents and winds need ballast and anchors'); regularly reflecting on how we are living, what provokes tension and stress within us and reviewing the day just passed through journaling and contemplation; reflecting and sharing with others with trust, integrity and authenticity (for instance, through techniques such as sharing circles, Way of Council, deep listening, constructive feedback, storytelling or coaching groups); noticing when we are harried and hurried, when we are stressed and ungrounded, catching any downward spirals of behavior before they develop too vigorously within us; learning what helps us re-connect, tune-in and cohere; taking time out regularly to reflect, review, rejuvenate and renew; sensing our natural rhythms and moods, and learning to work with these rather than suppressing them; cultivating our ability to sit in the uncomfortable space of 'not knowing' and not reacting to problems with premature solutions, instead pausing and embracing the spacious stillness to allow something deeper to emerge.

This self-recognizing is an on-going curious inquiry into what is going on within us at any given moment, and is not about getting absorbed in bouts of self-criticism. Essentially, it's an on-going checking-in with ourselves to sense our energies, motivations, coherence, priorities, values, behaviors, learnings and level of performance.

EXPERIMENTING

The core motive here is pushing our comfort zone through play. This exploration is about: upturning our assumptions; deliberately changing the dynamics or frames of perspective; being spontaneous, playful and creative; opening up to new ideas; innovating and collaborating in novel ways by embracing new techniques such as artful inquiry or applied improvisation; perceiving every conversation as a creative improvisational undertaking, an experiment that we invent spontaneously as we flow with the other; readiness to encounter unfamiliarity and upset with conviviality, creativity and compassion; seeing life itself as a series of experiments, as an on-going 'action research' project we embrace with openness, flexibility and adaptability while working toward practical outcomes with a spirit of inquiry, generosity, warmth and curiosity; life as a playground for being curious, imaginative and daring enough to envision a future with a fresh perspective by questioning all our assumptions.

> 'The important thing is not to stop questioning. Curiosity has its own reason for existing. One cannot help but be in awe when he contemplates the mysteries of eternity, of life, of the marvellous structure of reality. It is enough if one tries merely to comprehend a little of this mystery every day. Never lose a holy curiosity.'
> *Albert Einstein, genius*

These explorations put forward by Malcolm Parlett help us foster richer sense making amid challenging and stressful environments. In his words:

'When people, simultaneously, (1) are in touch both with their own needs in relation to the overall situation and also with 'what the situation requires of them' – and these are in alignment; (2) are engaging together with others, maintaining eye-contact, and 'following the dance between'; (3) are breathing fully and freely 'bodying forth' what they are experiencing, through body-positioning, gesturing, and possibly physical touch; (4) are letting go of feeling self-conscious, while also are not 'losing all sense of themselves' in some dissociated manner; and (5) are creatively adjusting to whatever is happening as the present unfolds, moving continuously between 'breaking new ground' and drawing on the solidity of what they know from past experience, something comes into existence that is almost beyond words, but is intensely felt...these times of whi-convergence can be celebratory, satisfying, full-bodied, and redolent of how life ought to be.' (Note 11)

To finish off this module on 'personal gnosis', here are some key attitudes that help buoy us as we cultivate our gnosis amid challenging work environments:

1. **GRATITUDE:** each day, each hour, each moment offers us fresh opportunity to remind ourselves of the beauty, abundance, creativity, wisdom and nourishment life provides. Granted, there are trials and tribulations, sufferings and scarcity, pains as well as pleasures in life, but underneath it all is an awesome utterly wonderful world: endless epic sunrises and sunsets; the menstruating moon framed by a multitude of glistening stars; ever transforming clouds of uniqueness; the ingeniousness of every blade of grass underfoot and leaf above our head; our heart pumping oxygenated blood to enrich every single cell in our body 100,000 times a day without fail; these are just a handful of reminders of our everyday wonder, much of which we take for granted without a second thought. As we remind ourselves of this, we cultivate our attitude of gratitude for simply being alive, experiencing this mind-boggling experience called Life. This attitude can brighten up our mood as we embrace the twists and turns, and stresses and strains of every-day.

2. **SURRENDER:** As contemporary philosopher Eckhart Tolle notes, surrender is the simple but profound wisdom of yielding to, rather than opposing, the flow of life. This is a remembering of our inter-relational being within this world beyond the fragmenting, anxiety-accumulating chatter of our ego-mind. In learning to let go of the incessant need to analyze, grasp at, define and rationalize, we may allow our being-in-the-world to just receptively 'be'. A relaxed yet at once alert and present attention of the moment, this is to surrender to life, unfettered by our own mental entrapment.

This surrendering is a self-emptying process which requires practice and patience. It is what the ancient Greeks, as well as Christian mystics including Jesus, understood as 'kenosis' (from the Greek verb 'kenosein' meaning 'to empty oneself' or 'to let go'). This kenosis is a state of being that allows us to become receptive to the flowing of Sophia within and all around us.

3. **TRUST:** As we surrender beyond the ego-mind we begin to permeate our sense of self with a deeper ecological awareness ('ecological' here meaning the inter-relational nature of life, with its physical interactions, energetic exchanges, psychical interplays and quantum resonances). We consciously engage with the deeper forces of life freed from the tendency to manipulate, control, analyze or define (due to our surrendering state of kenosis). This comes with vulnerability and intimacy, as well as a sense of inter-relational connectedness (a sense of inter-being). Here we call upon our trust in something greater, wiser and all-encompassing than our rationalizing ego-mind can grasp. The more we trust, the more we permeate, the more we engage, the more we open up, the more we give ourselves in service to something beyond our small individual sense of self. Our sense of self is still here yet it permeates with a deeper inter-relational awareness. (Note 12)

4. **COURAGE:** The word 'courage' comes from the Latin 'cor' which mean 'heart'. Courage is our embracing each moment with our hearts open. While we need our head as a useful assistant, it is through the heart that we open the door to our soul-awareness and align our bodymind in gnosis. Here we can begin to let go of codes of conduct, pre-determined outcomes and metrics of success, and surrender our 'need to know' while making space for a

wiser, deeper knowing to emerge through us. Opening up to our natural soul-awareness amid a volatile and challenging landscape requires courage.

5. HUMILITY: This opening up and being in service to something greater than our small individual self is what allows us to be humble as we accept our sense of place and purpose in this deeply wise world. This humble inner-sense ensures our outer ways of relating to others and the world is heartfelt and soulful. We attend with care rather than control, with soulful sociality rather than selfish separateness. 'Blessed are the meek, for they will inherit the Earth', said Jesus. The original Greek meaning of the word 'meek' finds its origins in 'praus' which means gentle humility, the opposite of hubris. As Gregory Bateson knew, it is hubris that undermines our greatness, and it is hubris that finds its origins in our sense of being separate from Nature, whereas humility flows from our sense of inter-being.

6. REVERENCE: This inner-sense and outer humility enables us to respect our selves, each other and the world around us, because we sense the sacredness of Nature, the Sophia running through life, the grace within each evolving moment, the love in another's eyes. No need for super-imposed dictate with hierarchies of control. And this is not to under-estimate the profound difference in knowing our path and walking our path (while knowing our path, we may still need to hang-on to the crutches of codes and charters before walking free yet continuously learning as we curiously explore the path with each humble step).

This is the Great Work that ancient traditions the world over point to and it comes with practice and patience, dedication and devotion. Learning to go easy with ourselves by recognizing mistakes as opportunities to learn helps us develop compassion for ourselves and others, as we are all in this together, each walking our path and offering ourselves in service to this Dance.

> 'And the day came when the risk to remain tight in a bud was more painful than the risk it took to blossom.'
> *Anais Nin, novelist*

Our aliveness is regenerative by its nature, it opens us up to the spiraling twists and turns, the yin-yang eddies, the breakdowns and breakthroughs inherent in life so that we can live more fully, more authentically, more artfully, more wisely. This aliveness involves plunging into the depths of suffering, death and rebirth as part-and-parcel of our own creative process – our poiesis. And yet, with a more soulful perspective, the suffering can be perceived for what it is - a springboard for a deeper unfurling of who we truly are.

In the same way, a poem, song, painting or film may provoke sadness within us, yet touch our soul, enriching our perspective and embracement of life in a way that allows us to widen our perceptual horizon, deepen our ways of knowing, and become more authentic in our presencing of life with its suffering and joy.

It is only through the ephemeral forms, feelings and conditions of life that we truly live: the eternal is creatively released within the ephemeral. And so we attain a deep soulful happiness not conditioned by negation of pain and suffering but through our opening up to life's rich weft.

TIP

STORY-TELLING

Recently, I co-hosted a Collaborative Inquiry with a group of thought-leaders from different disciplines. At the end of the first day together, we hosted a story-telling circle where everyone sat in a large circle and we went round the room spending three minutes each sharing a personal and intimate story of a moment in our lives when we experienced a shift in consciousness or momentary insight into how the challenges around sustainability, the evolution of human consciousness, and organizational transformation all aligned within our awareness. This simple exercise allowed for deep sharing amongst the participants while uncovering personal differences, deep synergies and an innate humanness we all share: our diversity within unity. And as Joanna Macy and Chris Johnstone note, 'when we share our cause with others, allies appear; synergy occurs.' [(Note 13)]

REFLECTIVE QUESTIONS

What do you most deeply and profoundly love?

What makes your heart break?

If all jobs paid the same, what would you do?

If you died tomorrow, what would your friends and relatives say about you at your funeral? What would you wish them to say about you – is there a difference, if so, what?

What are your top three strengths and top three weaknesses/areas of development?

What are your core values?

What are your biggest fears?

What do you fear most about the world you are leaving for the next generation?

What legacy do you wish to leave after you die?

If you could change one thing in the world, for definite, what would it be?

Can you find time in your weekly schedule to regularly incorporate some of the practices covered in this module?

MODULE **FIVE**

ORGANIZATIONAL GNOSIS

OUR PREVALENT CORPORATE CULTURE IS
INURED IN YESTERDAY'S LOGIC,
ENSLAVING OURSELVES, OUR TEAMS
AND ORGANIZATIONS IN WAYS THAT
UNDERMINE OUR HUMANITY. THE
GOOD NEWS IS THAT IN OPENING UP
TO A REGENERATIVE LOGIC, OUR
WORKPLACES, RELATIONSHIPS AND
CULTURES BECOME PURPOSEFUL,
PASSIONATE, COMPASSIONATE AND
CREATIVE PLACES.

EXECUTIVE SUMMARY

- Due to the world's inter-connecting epic problems, every organization now needs to take responsibility for moving toward regenerative business.

- Three important criteria in this shift toward regenerative business logic are: seeing systems; collaborating across boundaries; creating desired futures.

- Six 'ways of being' for organizational gnosis are: stillness, self-organizing, small steps, social, synchronicity, and soulful.

- These 'ways of being' infuse the firm of the future 'ways of doing' previously explored.

'THROUGHOUT THE AGES, PEOPLE HAVE SAID THAT THE WORLD IS IN THE MIDST OF BIG CHANGE. BUT THE LEVEL AND DEGREE OF GLOBAL CHANGE THAT WE FACE TODAY IS FAR MORE PROFOUND THAN AT ANY OTHER PERIOD IN MY ADULT LIFE. I CALL THIS PERIOD THE GREAT TRANSITION... I BELIEVE WE FACE A UNIQUE OPPORTUNITY. BECAUSE THE CHANGES WE FACE ARE SO PROFOUND THE DECISIONS WE MAKE WILL HAVE A DEEPER AND MORE LASTING IMPACT THAN PERHAPS ANY OTHER SET OF DECISIONS IN RECENT DECADES. WE HAVE NO TIME TO LOSE.'

BAN KI-MOON, UN SECRETARY GENERAL

THE INTER-CONNECTED GLOBAL AND LOCAL challenges affecting all our organizations demand urgent and systemic attention from each and every organization. At this stage there is little point in blaming others, pointing the figure or creating us-versus-them polarizations because the reality of our present predicament is that we are all in this together with every organization and stakeholder group able to play its part in creating and delivering value in ways that contribute to this Great Transition toward our regenerative future. For each organization, this is simultaneously an inner-organizational transformation – the organization and its employees transforming their ways of being and doing – and an inter-organizational transformation – the organization transforming the way it relates across it boundaries to co-create future-fit solutions with suppliers, customers, NGOs, local charities, pressure groups, communities, think tanks, public bodies and private institutions.

The business management specialist Peter Senge explores with others, in their book *The Necessary Revolution*, three legs of the stool essential for creating the learning capabilities needed to shift toward regenerative business: seeing systems; collaborating across boundaries; creating desired futures. (Note 1) Realizing each of these requires a fundamental shift in logic from our mechanistic mind-set; let's briefly explore these three legs in turn:

SEEING SYSTEMS: A major inhibitor to seeing and sensing the inter-relational systems of our business context is the dominant corporate culture which over-values short-term quantified financial metrics and personal achievement measured through these performance metrics. This undermines the resilience of our organizations. It's not that short-term performance metrics aren't useful, they are, as is ensuring short-term financial performance as part-and-parcel of healthy business continuity. Yet, if we dedicate too much time and energy to short-term financial success then it undermines our longer term viability as well as the intangible, non-quantifiable, yet valuable benefits attained through synergistic relations and reciprocities. Too narrow a lens, whether it's on short-term shareholder returns or next quarter's P&L figures, may help us get the immediate job done by reacting to challenges in quick yet superficial ways, but it over-looks the deeper systemic perspective we need for our shift to regenerative business.

COLLABORATING ACROSS BOUNDARIES: Our prevalent control-based and mechanistic logic is infatuated with measuring, monitoring and managing the atomized parts of our business while over-looking the inter-relationality of these parts within the wider context across team, business unit, organization and ecosystem boundaries. Parts become seen as discrete units to be separated into hierarchies of control and competition. This erodes the permeability and collaboration across boundaries along with the ability to explore shared visions and synergistic relations. This top-down containment and control of our natural sociality is the root of many of our organizational challenges. We find ourselves, on a day-to-day basis, involved in decision-making conventions that stifle rather than encourage our collaboration and openness. Rather than empowering people to get involved, contribute ideas, and work on problems in an inclusive and co-creative way, we tend toward tight management and control. In the pages ahead a number of simple yet powerful collaboration methods are offered as tips to help re-fertilize a collaborative corporate culture starting with our own meetings and conversations.

CREATING DESIRED FUTURES: Today's dominant management logic emphasizes tactical problem solving, incremental efficiency gains and short-term solution fixing, while not adequately balancing this with the creative endeavour of envisioning future scenarios that reach beyond business-as-usual. Our epic challenges demand that we enrich our risk-averse and reactionary mind-set with creative and collaborative systemic explorations that envision futures radically different from today.

In this module, we explore organizational 'ways of being' that fertilize the shift in logic now required by our firms of the future. The following 'ways of being' have been identified as foundational to cultivating this organizational gnosis: stillness, self-organizing, small steps, social, synchronicity, and soulful.

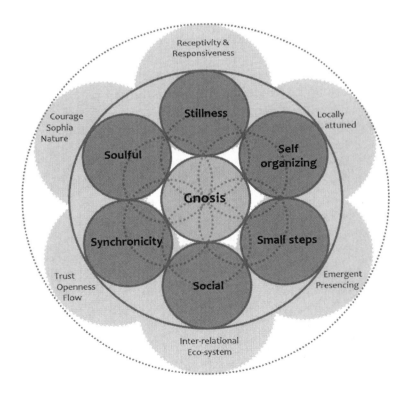

STILLNESS

Stillness is essential to our receptive quality of being. Stillness is not emptiness but intense awareness of 'what is'. It is not a cessation but a purity of attention which brings us into the aliveness of the here-and-now. Spontaneity is born from this stillness. Creativity spawns from this stillness. Scientific studies prove that our intuitive awareness needs a still, calm quality of attention.

> 'The wise are always at peace.'
> *Arab Proverb*

Learning to embrace the stillness within and all around us, through our attentive listening to what 'is', provides for the natural aliveness and creativity of our life-force to flow within us. As we invite this stillness into our awareness, we shift from attending to the surface of things into the deeper soulful nature emerging through our authentic relations. This stillness is both a personal and organizational quality, with our everyday conversations, meetings, corporate behaviors and approaches helping cultivate this stillness. After all, it is our rushing around from one thing to the next that gets us caught up in a vicious cycle of applying yesterday's logic to tomorrow's solutions. Our way out of this vicious cycle begins with embracing stillness within our work schedules and team dynamics.

We can learn to embrace this stillness through the way we speak, listen, and attend to each other as we go about our day. Are we rushing what we are saying? Are we projecting a honed narrative to get a point across or are we speaking from a deeper place? Are we truly listening to the other person or are we caught up in thoughts of how what they are saying affects me, my opinion and my world? When we say 'hello' to the person passing us in the corridor are we really present or simply too caught up in our own story and so just saying 'hello' out of habit?

Cultivating stillness in our everyday allows us to learn about and enhance our inner-outer dynamic through our relations with others. We can learn to sense how the inner noise (ego-chatter, churning emotions, anxieties about self-worth and status, unresolved arguments and frustrations, etc.) and outer noise (alarm clocks, emails pinging our inbox, automated repetitive station platform announcements, frustrated non-verbal exchanges during our commute to work, confrontational morning meetings, political backstabbing, etc.) can affect our ability to be fully present. This exploration of becoming intimate with stillness allows us to gain perspective on the situation and to sense the stillness within everything, beneath the surface of things. This stillness brings spaciousness into our day and brings a lightening-up of our mood and a general joyful, open receptivity, and deeper authenticity in our relating with others.

EXAMPLE: At the multi-media company, Sounds True, there is a minute's silence at the beginning of every meeting. We learn how best to use the minute's silence; not filling it with our monkey-mind masturbations or with practicing and honing how we are going to get our point across in the meeting, but space to let go and surrender from the head-chatter, to sense into the here-and-now and invite in the stillness. We prepare ourselves to be in service of the meeting, not beholden to our egos. One of us volunteers to be a guardian of the meeting by ringing a small bell when it is sensed that during the meeting someone is coming from a place of dominating ego-awareness. This acts as a gentle reminder to us all to catch ourselves and become more soulful, more receptive, responsive and reciprocating in our attention. The organization provides the frame for encouraging our personal gnosis, which enhances our ability to be in service of the organization rather than our egos: organizational gnosis enhances personal gnosis which enhances organizational gnosis; positive virtuous cycles form. (Note 2)

I once co-hosted a week long workshop exploring the emerging futures of business with eighteen participants. Every day, before we started the morning activities, and also before we started the afternoon activities, we all sat in a circle and a gong was sounded whereupon we all sat in silence for five minutes. Five minutes can seem like a long time for some participants who are not used to silent sitting or meditation, yet by mid-week all participants had become not just comfortable with it, but actually felt it a necessary perquisite to having a constructive learning and sharing session. Similarly, at a Quakers & Business Conference I recently spoke at, we sat for about twenty minutes at the beginning of the day in silence. This allowed us all to enter into the spirit of the day with receptive, soulful awareness. The Quakers, as a matter of course, have silent time at the beginning and end of every meeting, allowing participants to centre themselves at the start and end of all group discussions. Could you imagine bringing in such a simple yet powerful routine into your organization? Try it out; you might be surprised at the response from people, as we all urgently need more stillness in our work schedules. Far from it getting in the way of performance, it greatly enhances it. No budget required.

SELF-ORGANIZING

The more soulful we become, the more our teams and wider organizational culture can let go of the hierarchic command-and-control structures in place. Self-organizing ways of working are now becoming more accepted across all sectors and sizes of business, with a variety of organizations applying formalized approaches for self-organization such as Holacracy, Scrum and Sociocracy or developing their own home-grown approaches. Ex-Mckinsey consultant Frederic Laloux in his well-received book *Reinventing Organizations* explores how different organizations are successfully applying their own styles of self-organization, for instance Buurtzorg the non-profit healthcare organization in the Netherlands and Morning Star the food processing manufacturer in America. (Note 3)

The more we recognize the importance of our 'ways of being' infusing our 'ways of doing', the more our relationship dynamics - listening and collaborating skills, personal accountability and facilitation skills - allow for team decision-making without the need for over-bearing control-based hierarchies. Similarly, the more our organizational culture allows self-organization to be tried out, the more we are able to learn how to operate effectively in teams without over-bearing hierarchies in place. It takes time for people to get used to such a radically different way of operating, where we all take personal responsibility and accountability for making decisions in groups without the boss looking over our shoulder. And we learn through experimenting and practicing, being patient with ourselves and each other as we get used to being empowered, having a voice and taking direct responsibility for decisions and their implementation. This helps provide enthusiasm amongst the team - our fuel for journeying toward becoming creative, passionate, purposeful firms of the future.

Experienced coaching is vital in the early stages while teams are learning to feel their way as control-hierarchies are relaxed. Coaching is also an important on-going function as part of the overall governance to allow teams to check-in every so often with local and regional coaches who provide unbiased advice on how to best transcend tensions and challenges. These coaches can be full-time employees of the organization or external consultants, or a mix of both. Likewise, training in communication skills, team dynamics, facilitation, deep listening, peer-coaching, open-ended questioning, conflict transformation, non-violent communication, etc. greatly assists all team members rising to the challenge of self-organization. Conflict and tension is inevitable; the trick is learning how to transform it in constructive ways.

Some people will not be able to embrace such a way of working and may find it better to leave that area of the business or the organization all together, others will flourish and show a natural flair for becoming facilitators across the business and most of us will struggle, but learn and improve as we go. It is only through struggling and learning that teams develop into high performing self-organizing teams – nothing worthwhile comes easy in life. By example, I recently spent time with a CEO of an organization that is viewed as conscious and ethical when compared with its peers, and yet the organization has failed to effectively embrace self-organizing techniques across its business for a variety of reasons. The CEO remarked that one key reason why the organization failed was due to a lack of good quality internal and external facilitators to call upon when struggles and challenges inevitably occurred. The CEO also recognized that a certain threshold of emotional maturity and conscious awareness needs to be in place within the teams if self-organizing is to work well without regular interventions from 'above'. Allowing this emotional maturity and conscious awareness to develop across an organization takes time and commitment.

Each organization (and team) needs to explore ground rules that encourage a context where self-organization can thrive without too much direction setting from 'above'. These can be general behaviors set across the business to help guide the teams, like a moral compass. Buurtzorg, for instance, has set the rule that teams should not grow larger than twelve people and that care should be taken to ensure tasks are widely dispersed amongst all team members to avoid a creep toward hierarchy or informal power bases. At the Brazilian manufacturer, Semco, team members regularly provide 360 degree feedback to each other ensuring tensions do not build unnecessarily. At the French manufacturer, FAVI, each self-organizing team is dedicated to a specific customer and each team is responsible for forming their own rules of engagement with terms of reference and performance criteria continuously adapting to customers' requirements, yet everyone across the organization is trained in ground rules that encourage healthy collaborative workplaces. (Note 4)

> 'Things get done around here, without drama, and with clarity and regenerative creativity. The *esprit de corps* is very positive and sustaining – not because we're uniquely optimistic, but because the system in which we operate is healthy and liberates our energies to flow and function.'
> *Deborah Boyar, HolacracyOne employee*

The more open, transparent and trusting the environment, the more we can start to flow in a soulful inter-relational way. This is nothing more than opening up to our natural humanity as collaborative, creative, sharing beings. We all essentially want to partake in meaningful soul-fulfilling work in service of something beyond ourselves, while being empowered to take part in the decision making, and responsibly playing our part within healthy, vibrant team work. Yet, many of us might well prefer to stick to the conventional approach of limited empowerment within a clear hierarchic structure, so inured we have become in yesterday's logic. And that's absolutely fine. We need to be conscious of how best to push forward radical transformation in our ways of working while nurturing, coaching and guiding people as we venture forward.

TIP

CONSTRUCTIVE FEEDBACK

During my years as a management consultant for KPMG I was fortunate to attend a great variety of world-class training and development courses. One of the most memorable courses I attended was on how to give and receive feedback. I learnt that giving and receiving feedback is a present, a reciprocating gift that nourishes both the giver and receiver. It is not about critically judging the other, or a veiled form of ego one-upmanship, it is about authentically wishing to help the other by providing useful insights into what has gone well and not-so-well from our empathic perspective, therefore allowing the receiver to identify areas of learning and development.

When giving feedback in this way, we sit in pairs across from each other, maintaining relaxed and friendly eye contact throughout. We start off with a positive 'what went well' feedback comment to help create an open, sharing and friendly environment. We can all feel apprehensive and defensive about receiving feedback no matter how constructive it is to our development, and so creating an empathic atmosphere is important. Then we alternate between giving a positive comment and constructive feedback on what did not go so well or could be improved upon. We need to frame our words carefully and constructively, empathizing with how it feels to receive such feedback, positioning it as a gift, a useful insight to help the other. Giving examples or referring to specific situations or conversations rather than generalities helps the receiver better perceive the problem and sense into what could have worked better. It is best if the receiver simply listens and takes notes to allow the giver to go through all comments without interruption, yet the receiver can ask for clarification or further expansion, as opposed to starting to justify why what was done was done – this is not about justifying ones actions, as important as that may seem to our ego, this is about taking on-board someone else's perspective and insight which is being shared in the spirit of helping us learn. Three 'positives' and two 'learning areas' per feedback session is enough for us to digest and work with. Then the partners can rotate with the receiver now becoming the person giving the feedback and the other person listening, clarifying and taking notes; alternatively it may not be suitable or necessary to rotate.

The more we build-in regular cycles of feedback within our teams, the more we are able to sense and respond, adapt and learn, without the need for over-arching decision-making. We can start to embed informal spontaneous feedback as part of our normal daily undertaking of business. The gift of feedback deepens the authenticity and wisdom of both the giver and receiver and also the wider team's relational dynamics. The 'giving' is also a 'receiving'; a sacred reciprocity where we give simply to nourish the other and nourish the matrix of relations we operate in, as a result it nourishes ourselves as it enriches our communal context. Our personal gnosis (through soulful giving) enriches the organizational gnosis (team dynamics and organizational learning) which in turn enriches our personal gnosis (the context we find ourselves in is more giving, reciprocating, authentic and soulful, allowing us to further open up through vulnerability and deeper learning).

EXAMPLE: A large sales organization created a 'best failure' ritual as part of each Monday morning staff meeting, where employees volunteer to share any learning from the previous week with the rest of the team. The person who shares the 'best failure' receives a funny prize and a round of applause for contributing to the overall learning of the team. (Note 5)

Essentially, this is all about creating and nurturing soulful working spaces where we feel safe enough to allow our soulful awareness to emerge. As Frederic Laloux notes, 'many of the corporate ills today can be traced to behaviors driven by fearful egos: politics, bureaucratic rules and processes, endless meetings, analysis paralysis, information hoarding and secrecy, wishful thinking, ignoring problems away, lack of authenticity, silos of infighting, decision-making concentrated at the top'. Self-organizing teams require our egos to be tamed and for inevitable conflict and tension to be dealt with in constructive, healthy ways. This is all easier said than done, and it is through practice, good facilitation and commitment across the organization that self-organizing teams can start to perform.

EXAMPLE: The fast-growing on-line retailer Zappos has a fascinating approach to developing a self-organizing culture through fostering collaboration and happiness. It pays new recruits $2,000 to quit if they wish, makes customer service the responsibility of the entire company, and operates through non-hierarchic 'holacratic' governance where everyone is involved in the decisions related to their area. Everyone takes responsibility for their own skill-set and pace of learning, setting their own training schedule related to their ambitions. On Friday's people share stories of other people they wish to thank for things they have done during the week, and prizes are given out. There are off-site sessions and retreats where people are encouraged to share their inner-selves with others in their teams in convivial and relaxed environments. Zappos is regularly listed as one of the world's best companies to work for, and sees delivering happiness as core to its mission.

EXAMPLE: Quite different from Zappos, yet just as radical in its humanity, is Semco, a Brazilian-based manufacturer with over 3,000 workers. It is often called one of the most interesting companies in the world. There are no job titles, no written policies, no HR department, and no headquarters. There is still a CEO, but half a dozen senior executives pass the title every six months. All other employees are Associates. Twelve levels of hierarchy have been reduced down to three. People set their own salaries and working hours. Everybody shares in the profits. Everyone in the company knows what everyone else does. Every employee receives the company's financial statements and can take classes on how to read them. Team members choose their managers by vote and evaluate them through publicly posted results. Meetings are voluntary, and two seats at every board-meeting are open to the first employees who turn up.

Semco and Zappos join a growing number of companies transforming toward a more participatory, self-organizing, emergent way of working bonded by strong culture, a spirit of sharing, conviviality, passion and personal responsibility.

While these examples are inspiring for us, the reality is that most workplaces operate in survival mode these days. A mode of fear and competition rather than happiness and collaboration permeates our corridors of power, along with a constant anxiety to do things, horde information for our own benefit, and play politics, while eyeing-up our corporate world through threat-tinted glasses.

> 'Seeing a turbulent world through threat-tinted glasses invites the dysfunctions of threat rigidity – centralized control, limited experimentation, and focus on existing resources – that stymies the pursuit of opportunity.'
> *Donald Sull, professor of strategy*

We all have fears, and fear is very natural and important for us as humans. Fear can help us hold back, check things out before diving in, helping us avoid disastrous scenarios. Yet, if fear is allowed to dominate the way we attend to the world, our relationships are undermined and our ability to adapt, develop, grow, learn, and add-value erodes. Fear can be the biggest obstacle to our take-up of self-organizing, soulful ways of working; and many of our fears are culturally embedded into our organizational context and wider socio-economic worldview. If we are honest with ourselves, we might see that our fears drive much of our behavior in and out of the workplace; but, this does not have to be the case. An important part of our personal and organizational gnosis is liberating ourselves and our cultural context from these ingrained fears.

In opening up to and naming our fears, both personally and organizationally, we can start to see beyond them, allowing them to be instructive rather than destructive. The more we learn to be conscious of our fears, the more awareness we have of them and the more we can see them for what they are, useful indicators as opposed to obstacles blocking our growth.

TIP

NAMING OUR FEARS

Let us take a moment to pause, breathe deep and relax. Now let's spend a few moments reflecting and writing down the three things we really fear in our life right now. We just jot down the first things that come into our head without too much analysis. Then we look at them and see them for what they are.

This activity can also be effective in groups of people. Once I hosted a workshop for ninety senior business people and asked them all to reflect on their fears in silence for a few moments. I then invited people to share what came to them. After a few tentative shares from the bolder members of the group, more and more people were willing to share. Soon it was apparent to the group that we all share quite similar underlying fears, such as: the fear of being thought a failure; the fear of not living up to our potential; the fear of dying without achieving what we were born to achieve; the fear of being judged by others or ourselves as 'not good enough'; the fear of not being loved or accepted by others, etc..

This sharing helps us see how we are all in this together, all seeking forms of acceptance and love from others and yet also noticing how we often judge ourselves and others critically, and so actually contributing to the very situation we are fearful of.

This simple exercise of naming and sharing our fears helps us empathize with others; lightening up about our own fears, while developing a more compassionate outlook. A similar exercise can be done individually, in pairs or in groups, exploring what makes us joyful, alive, passionate and purposeful, as well as fearful. Again, quite quickly it becomes apparent we all share similar core underlying drivers around what makes us joyful. This open sharing of our fears and joys within our work teams helps create the conditions conducive for collaborative self-organizing teams to flourish.

EXAMPLE: Richard Sheridan is CEO of Menlo Innovations, an organization which now receives over 2,500 visitors a year just to see how the company works. Having become disillusioned after spending years in traditional organizations, Sheridan was determined to set up his own company based on the founding principle that work can be joyful and that an organization can be a community of joy. In fact, the story of Menlo Innovations, made famous through Sheridan's book *Joy Inc.*, is proving that joy at work is actually good business sense because it makes the company more profitable, more desirable to work for, more innovative and more adaptive. As Sheridan notes, 'when you walk into the room you feel the joy.' With the underpinning principle of joy in place, a self-organizing culture forms quite naturally at Menlo, with two people working to one computer, everyone switching work-pairs regularly, and meetings forming spontaneously without calendars to schedule them. Sheridan's journey started with himself, by exploring how to best serve what was in his own heart, and through that he embarked on creating an environment that served the joy of others. (Note 6)

SMALL STEPS

A firm of the future has a mission, vision and plan, yet recognizes that the art of regenerative business is our skilful adaptation to the ever-changing landscape. This is best achieved through continual cyclic iterations (remember the 'adaptive cycle' of living systems) continuously testing new things out, innovating and prototyping, exploring what works best and what does not. It is what many of the Silicon Valley start-ups have mastered - they call it 'learning to fail fast'. The more we fail, the more we learn, and the more we succeed.

So, at one level, 'small steps' is about how we place new steps of change amid continual adaptation and learning. Yet, it is also about the 'way' in which we place our new steps of change: the everyday interactions within our organization, whether it be our collaborating during a meeting, sharing with our stakeholder partners, conversing with our team members, or listening and speaking with a colleague next to the coffee machine or in the boardroom or on a conference call. As the adage goes 'it's not what you do, it's the way that you do it!'

We learn to feel into the way we are being. Can we sense when the 'way' we are interacting is more soulful (receptive-responsive-reciprocity) and how different this feels from a more domineering, judging, reacting or manipulating way? Our self-recognition is important here as we learn to place these small steps in a soulful way amid the busyness of everyday work-life.

> 'We cannot do great things; we can only do small things
> with great love'
> *Mother Teresa, healer*

Small steps with great love – this is the motto of the firm of the future. Learning to catch ourselves in-the-moment and reflect; noticing how we are listening to the other, how we are speaking, sharing, sensing and responding. This is the front line of it all, where 'the rubber hits the road'.

I am reminded by a graceful facilitator I have had the pleasure of working with, Genevieve Boast, that as well as this being about how we 'walk-our-talk' - leading by example by putting our principles into practice through our everyday interactions - it is also about how we 'talk-our-walk' - conversing and co-learning with others as we walk these small steps, sharing insights about how we can improve upon things, feeding-back on how we are feeling, checking-in with others for further clarity and deeper sharing.

EXAMPLE: The French manufacturer FAVI applies a simple technique to its daily work schedule which helps provide a convivial atmosphere conducive to sharing. At the beginning of every meeting there is a round-robin where people volunteer stories of someone in the organization (or stakeholder ecosystem) they would like to thank. It is a simple way of encouraging an atmosphere of gratitude and sharing, encouraging our being-in-service to others rather than in service of our own ego-agendas. (Note 7)

Zappos the American on-line retailer does a similar thing every Friday, encouraging people to share stories of where people have helped others. (Note 8) A UK media company I know has team check-ins at the beginning and end of every day where small groups huddle round in circles and openly share what's on their mind, providing informal feedback to each other while sharing what they feel is working well and what could be improved upon. This informal, self-organizing medium allows people to get things off their chest before leaving the office for the day, and in the morning it allows people to share insights or concerns that have come to them over night. There is no line-management authority trying to maintain control, no agenda or planned objective, just a group of people sharing in a human way, it's as simple as that.

>᠆᠆᠆

One of the most essential of human qualities is our heartfelt relating with others. Yet, so often in today's mind-set we find ourselves very far from this kind of communication. For instance, how often do we really listen to the other person with all of our attention, without getting distracted with thoughts of past or future, or how what is being said affects me and my priorities for the day. To truly listen to the other is a vital 'small step' toward developing our firm of the future. Techniques such as deep listening, non-violent communication and Way of Council can help us cultivate this attentiveness so that we can learn to walk our personal and collective paths with loving, attentive, conscious steps.

TIP

WAY OF COUNCIL

Through the ancient practice of Way of Council groups of people come together to share within a communal atmosphere of non-judgment and acceptance. In Council, people sit in a circle and commit to being fully present, freed from distractions, judgements or opinion forming, listening intently and sharing open-heartedly with each other without preparing or rehearsing our responses.

There is a beacon or talking-piece (which may be a stick, a stone, a ball or whatever feels appropriate). The person holding the beacon artefact is the only one allowed to speak, everyone else round the circle listens with complete attention and presence. Then, when the talking-piece is put back in the centre or passed round the circle, the next person to hold it speaks, knowing they will not be interrupted or judged. Here are some basic ground rules:

- When speaking, we speak from our heart and gut, not from our head. We do not rehearse what we are going to say, we allow what comes up within us to come out. We talk from the 'I' perspective, about what is going on for 'me', not using words such as 'you' or 'they', and we do not bring in blame or projection on to others. We simply talk about what is going on for me, how I am feeling and the challenges or opportunities I am experiencing. This 'first person' speaking allows us to take responsibility for what we are feeling and saying without accusing, judging or projecting. We are also conscious of the time available for the circle, by being concise in our speech and not rambling too much or speaking for too long.

- When listening, we listen with our whole bodymind, being present in the here-and-now, so that our attention is fully absorbed in listening generously and open-heartedly to what is being said. The act of listening in such a deep and fully present way is beneficial in-and-of-itself as the act of listening to another helps us remain mindful, embodied and present. We catch ourselves when thoughts of past or future distract us, and when emotions or judgements triggered by what we are listening to form in us along with associated thought patterns. We continuously bring ourselves back to the act of fully listening each time our attention wanders. This helps keep our heart open and also helps a social field of collective wisdom to resonate within the group, which further enhances our heart-felt listening and speaking. This attentive listening is powerful and cleansing for everyone in the circle.

- There is a natural ego-tendency to wish to rehearse what we are going to say, so we come across as fluent and intelligible, our ego not wanting to trust what might

emerge from our heart and gut. But, we let go of the
ego-grasping desire to rehearse. This helps us build trust
in our other ways of knowing beyond the rationalizing
head. It also frees us to be fully present in the moment
and enjoy being here-and-now, listening attentively, rather
than rehearsing in our head while others speak. When we
speak from this deeper heart and gut place a more
cathartic and soulful sharing occurs, which enriches us
personally and the circle collectively. We may well feel
fear when it's our turn to take the talking-piece, our ego
afraid that what may come out will be critically judged by
others. This is part-and-parcel of trusting ourselves and
trusting the circle of people who are dedicated to being
open and attentive as best we all can be without judging,
just listening. This learning not to rehearse while having
trust, is a surrendering process, a form of 'kenosis', by
letting go of pre-defining thoughts to allow something
deeper to emerge. It is a great way for us to practice
becoming more comfortable at bringing in more of our
soul-awareness into our work-life.

- The talking-piece acts as a beacon of attention. Our
  attention follows the talking-piece and we give whoever
  has it our full attention.

- No criticism or judgement about other's sharing. We do
  not critically analyze what another has just shared when
  we come to speak, yet we may refer to another's comment
  in terms of how it affects 'me' and my feelings. So we
  share how what has been said relates to what is going on
  for 'me' without getting dragged into me-versus-you
  judgements or criticisms. This helps cultivate self-
  recognition within us; helping us notice when we are
  tending to blame, defend or project as opposed to

open-heartedly sharing what is going on for me without projecting on to others.

- Silence is always permitted while holding the talking-piece, and we can pass it on without saying anything at all if we wish.

- What is said in the circle stays in the circle. General themes may be captured and shared by means of informing our work in general, but people's specific sharing remains confidential and not specifically quoted beyond the circle without permission. This especially relates to gossip. Learning to respect the confidentiality of the circle by holding back on gossiping about others is once again an important learning for us, teaching us to respect each other's perspectives and become more self-aware about our tendency to gossip.

As a practice, Council is applicable to all social interrelations from family discussions to executive board meetings. For indigenous cultures, where collective decisions are regularly made through this circle of shared dialogue, it is acceptance rather than consensus which is paramount – an empathic understanding of the differing views occurs even if everyone is not in agreement with the final decision. This way resentment does not build up and then corrode the community. Differing opinions are healthy and ought to be celebrated as it is diverse opinions within a community that provide for the resilience needed for long term viability. (Note 9)

This ancient communication method of Way of Council is similar to the more recent techniques of non-violent communication (Note 10) and Dialogue (Note 11). Both Dialogue and non-violent communication are simple yet profound approaches to communication now widely used in business situations to great effect. These techniques are aimed at helping us stay in touch with our authentic selves while embracing deep listening, empathy and non-judgemental conversation. This is all aimed at helping us notice and curb our ego-reactions while bringing in deeper receptivity and compassion amid our often stressful work environment. With practice, we learn to replace our ego-patterns of defending, judging, blaming, withdrawing, manipulating or attacking with a deeper natural compassion and innate human desire to share from the heart with authenticity.

EXAMPLE: The furniture design company, Herman Miller, has won many Best Company awards, as well as being listed in Fortune as one of the Top Ten most environmentally responsible corporations. At the heart of its operational and ethical success is a reliance on Dialogue as a way of embedding authentic communications throughout the organization and wider stakeholder ecosystem.

Through an on-going process of Dialogue, supported by participative and transparent communications systems, Herman Miller ensures rich, authentic conversations about what matters most for people across the organization is not a one-off 'corporate project' but an alive, continuous process. Key to this is a deep understanding of what Dialogue really feels like in practice: deep listening, empathy, open-hearted sharing.

Over several months, ninety-six senior executives and managers from across the organization received off-site coaching on the art of Dialogue, and then immersed themselves in smaller group Dialogue sessions about company values and what it means to live these values on a day-to-day basis. These ninety-six leaders then engaged their teams through empathic, heart-felt and thought-provoking conversations. Cross-functional action teams cross-fertilized these conversations while making recommendations on how to close the gap between proposed values and day-to-day reality. This on-going process enriches the organization from the inside out, helping it be an ethical, innovative and financially successful market leader. (Note 12)

SOCIAL

While we learn a great deal from cultivating our inner-sense, the more aware we become the more we realize how our 'self' is immersed within a social web of inter-relations, human and more-than-human. The 'self' is inherently social, there is no separation. We are social creatures with an innate ability to socialize, empathize, collaborate and adapt as communities of people within an ever-changing web of contextual relations. As the psychotherapist, John Welwood insightfully notes, 'We don't often see that how we relate to another inevitably follows from how we relate to ourselves, that our outer relationships are but an extension of our inner life, that we can only be as open and present with another as we are with ourselves.' (Note 13)

Likewise, our creative potential and fulfilment as individuals is entwined with the culture and relational logic of the organization, which in turn flourishes through our diverse individuality and inter-relationality. We - as individuals, teams, organizations, and stakeholder ecosystems - fully embrace and acknowledge differences by understanding a variety of perspectives through authentic communication (listening and speaking from the heart). We each take responsibility for helping encourage wise meetings where we share authentically, spontaneously and creatively with each other and get to the heart of the matter by reaching past our self-serving ego power-plays and projections. The more intimate we learn to be

with ourselves, the more intimate we can learn to be
with others.

TIP

STAKEHOLDER DIALOGUE INTERVIEWS

In today's world, we need to work collaboratively with a diverse
array of stakeholders with different agendas and drivers.
Through stakeholder dialogue meetings - as either one-on-one
stakeholder interviews or group discussions - we can encourage a
healthy collaborative relationship to form by exploring any
concerns and potential for synergies in a relaxed,
conversational way.

This meeting is an opportunity for trust to develop while any
initial apprehensions or tensions can be eased through listening,
empathy and receptive sharing. It is important that we enter
such an initial meeting with an open state of mind - a learning
attitude rather than a fixed agenda or specific outcome in mind.

So, in preparing for the meeting, we try not to load ourselves up
with lots of questions (as useful as this may seem) as lots of
questions may make others defensive or suspicious. Rather, we
have some main areas sketched out that we would like to explore.
The most important thing is to spend adequate time just before
the interview cultivating stillness within us so that we are in a
receptive, open state of mind for the meeting. According to
stakeholder dialogue specialist Joseph Jaworski, up to an hour of
meditation prior to the meeting is highly recommended, within
which we let go of any pre-defined goals or desired outcomes
and simply relax so that we are present, conscious and receptive

for what will emerge in the meeting. [Note 14] Then we undertake the meeting in an open and flowing way, following the natural flow of where the conversation takes us, letting go of preconceived outcomes or objectives and instead creating a good foundation for future dialogue and collaboration. Let's take a moment here to explore qualities that can enhance this heartfelt dialogue.

Dialogue recognizes the importance of conversation as a listening, feeling, learning, sharing dynamic. The famous quantum physicist David Bohm in his later years became passionate about the benefits of Dialogue as a way to enhance the richness of human communication, and he formulated an approach to Dialogue which has since been adapted and enhanced by several practitioners.

Based on their extensive experience of working with Dialogue, Chris Laszlo and Judy Sorum Brown, in their book *Flourishing Enterprise,* provide some guidance:

- Begin with a powerful question, for instance, 'What draws you toward the goal of becoming a regenerative business?'

- Shift from knowing to wondering. It is OK to be uncertain, to question and explore as this opens up exploratory ground, rather than holding-on to preconceived definitive perspectives;

- Shift from statements to thought-provoking questions that draw out interest in the other;

- Shift from certainty to curiosity, develop a genuinely curious interest about the topic and what is emerging, letting go of any pre-conceived notions about what is right or not;

- Speak only for ourselves and about our own experience, from a grounded heartfelt presence of where we are right now;

- Resist the temptation to get sucked into to-and-fro 'tennis match' debates, exploratory questions can help dissolve a debate;

- Listen (inside and out) with intense curiosity while suspending our assumptions, giving up the ego-need to hear ourselves speaking or hear someone agreeing with what we have said, and notice any internal tensions forming in ourselves without allowing them to disrupt our dialogue;

- Allow for silence. Silence can be productive and generative while allowing us to take in what has been said and let-go of urges to react;

- Listen generously and deeply;

- Seek and welcome difference without getting sucked into debate, as difference sharpens our collective exploration and learning;

- Speak with a fresh voice, resist saying what we might normally respond with, remaining silent if need be until we have something genuine to offer, and do not interrupt others;

- Bring 100% of ourselves with complete attention and presence, letting go of distractions and frustrations. [Note 15]

As we develop our self-recognition, awareness and personal mastery, we learn to open up and commune with others in a more authentic way, recognizing that the way we share and relate with others forms part of the rich matrix of relations that affects all life including ourselves. It is here that we understand the wisdom of 'loving thy neighbor as thy self'.

TIP

DEEP LISTENING

We find a partner to pair up with for this exercise (a team member or stakeholder we are working with, or even our spouse or neighbor). We sit opposite each other, get comfortable, relax, and warmly look at each other in the eyes. We aim to maintain this eye contact throughout this exercise. One person is going to speak first, for three minutes, and the other person is going to listen without interrupting. Then we are going to swap over, with the other person speaking for three minutes.

We can explore personal reflective questions such as: What do I most deeply and profoundly love? What would I like to change about my life? What are my greatest fears? Or, we can explore work related questions such as: What is really concerning me at the moment at work? How do I feel about the changes afoot in my work area? If I could change two things about my work-life what would they be? What is holding me back from improving my work-life? If I could have any job within the organization what would it be and why?

What is the deepest and most profound purpose my organization ought to have?

If time allows, it is great to start with general personal questions first and then explore more specific work related questions in further rounds. Once the pair is clear on the question they are going to speak about, they agree who is going to speak first for three minutes, while the other listens attentively and fully.

The listener should refrain from any bodily queues that could influence the speaker such as smiling, frowning or nodding. We listen with a blank yet open and warm expression and maintain eye contact throughout. We remain aware of how present we are while listening, catching ourselves when caught up in distractions, or thoughts about what is being said. We keep bringing our attention back to fully listening. As said before, this act of listening is a form of meditation in itself as it helps us free ourselves from ego-chatter. This helps us become more receptive. The speaker will, either consciously or unconsciously, sense this deeper awareness opening up between us allowing for a deepening of authentic heart-felt sharing.

The speaker knows there is space to say whatever comes up without fear of interruption or judgement. When we are speaking it is important for us to tune into our bodymind, feeling into our heart and gut to sense what wants to be spoken through us with regard to the question. This is not about answers or right or wrong responses, this is a general inquiry and whatever comes up is absolutely fine. This helps the speaker cultivate somatic awareness while speaking; learning to listen to the heart and gut and how this informs us. We speak spontaneously and freely as we go with pauses and spaces for stillness as-and-when it feels right. It does not matter if the speaker says little or gets into a flow and pours out a lot, nothing is right or wrong here and all is beyond judgement.

The facilitator calls time after three minutes (or if no facilitator, the listener calls time). Then there are a few seconds of stillness before we swap over. In this space between swapping over, the pair can show gratitude, smile, and say thank you before the next session starts, and the process is repeated over again.

This deep listening practice can also be adapted for three people, where we still share as a pair sitting opposite each other with a third person taking notes and then providing feedback at the time of change over. We rotate round until each of the three people have taken part in all of the activities (listening, feeding-back, speaking).

This practical embodied experience of reciprocated sharing is a great way to start embedding personal and organizational gnosis into the organization. It requires no training or budget, just some basic ground rules, yet has a profound impact.

TIP

CULTIVATING OUR LISTENING SKILLS THROUGHOUT THE DAY

Deep listening can be consciously brought into how we listen and engage throughout the day in all our meetings and conversations. When we are in a meeting, we can catch ourselves, notice how we are being, what is going on in our head, the type of inner-dialogue, the judgements, the frustrations, and opinions that form in us. We can make a note on this either mentally or jotting it down, journaling as we go.

We can utilize every interaction as a practice to sense into when we are actually being fully present, really tuning-in to what is being said with our full attention, and when we are allowing judgements, emotions, distractions, and such like, to fill our awareness. When we sense this ego-chatter, we may ask ourselves the following exploratory questions: Am I judging others? Am I rehearsing what I am going to say? Am I getting caught up in ruminating head-chatter? Or am I being receptive to 'what is'? Can I sense all my ways of knowing, my intuition, my felt-senses, my emotional intelligence as well as what is going on in my thinking head? Can I allow myself to sense a deeper stillness beneath the noise of my thoughts and feelings? What can I pick up and tune-in to beyond my immediate thoughts and judgements? The more we practice this self-awareness throughout our work day, the more we cultivate a deepening of 'knowing thy self'.

EXAMPLE: One of the world's largest banking corporations, HSBC, wanted to develop a renewed sense of purpose and community for its 250,000 people across 72 countries. In a company-wide programme referred to as 'join the conversation', senior leaders and local managers convene small groups of 10-15 people and listen in silence to what really matters most to employees. Three years since inception it continues to evolve in different and unexpected ways and is now widely recognized across the organization as bringing humanity back into the workplace by engendering a culture where employees listen to each other more readily and deeply.

Emmajane Varley, Global Head of Communications for HSBC, notes that through the simple act of senior leaders listening in silence while employees talk, meaningful conversations and collaboration spawn. The leaders and local managers take responsibility for taking notes during the 'conversation', writing up their notes on the intranet afterward so all employees can read through and see what the leaders captured, picked-up and learnt. Following on from these listening sessions, themes for conversations develop which local groups can then explore further.

We are now going to dive into a series of powerful methods for holding meetings that break the command-and-control mentality of our current corporate conventions by empowering our people to collaborate in self-organizing emergent ways. Then, we will move on to the other organizational 'ways of being' – synchronicity and soulful.

TIP

STORY CAFÉ AND WORLD CAFÉ

This is a simple yet effective way of hosting small groups (story café) or large groups (world café) in dialogue. We gather a group of stakeholders around tables of four seats per table (no more than five per table) and start by discussing a topic that everyone feels involved in. The discussion itself follows a dialogue approach, in terms of listening intently and sharing in an open and heartfelt way. Let's say we start with the discussion: 'Share a time when we felt fully alive in our lives'; each of us sharing a short story about it.

At the beginning of the discussion, when everyone is clear on the question or topic being discussed, we start the process with a minute's silence and also perhaps some conscious breathing to develop our conscious awareness and receptivity. Then each person, in silence, jots down their own story. After three minutes of this, the first person shares their story within the table of four, the other three listen attentively, without interruption, like we practiced in the deep listening exercise. After three minutes we move round the table with another person sharing their story and the other three listening attentively. We repeat, until everyone has shared.

We have no need to sell our stories or present them in inauthentic ways, although to start with there may be that tendency, as we wish to make ourselves look good in front of others, but as we gain experience in this kind of sharing our desire to put on a show dissipates as our deeper authenticity starts to come through. We learn first-hand the importance of this sharing as a gift where it deepens our perspectives of ourselves and others while increasing our team empathy, reciprocity and wisdom. As we get more comfortable with this authentic sharing, we may wish to discuss questions related to the challenges in our organization, for instance, sharing what makes us really alive in our work-place and how we might encourage more of it.

With World Café, we have a large group with more than two or three tables of people and, after a couple of rounds of discussion amongst the tables, people are free to leave their table and join another table where space allows. A table host stays on the table but all others are free to move around to experience slightly different sharing with different people. The questions evolve as the session develops. The hosts then share the insights with the overall group.

EXAMPLE: Scott Bader, a multinational chemicals company, recently applied World Café as an approach to engaging colleagues and enriching its culture through what it termed 'Cultural Cafés'. Since its inception in 1921, Scott Bader has cherished a culture of engaging its people, encouraging them to bring their whole selves to work, while providing benefit for future generations.

With its recent Cultural Cafés approach, where people internally were trained as facilitators, the company aimed to reinvigorate colleague engagement by running sessions across the global operations. Colleagues explored what is different about Scott Bader, the benefits of its democratic governance approach, and what individuals and the company could do to improve things. These Cafés helped gather vital information from teams across the global organization which then helped shape global and local initiatives for colleagues to buy in to.

TIP

OPEN SPACE TECHNOLOGY

This is a powerful way to run self-organizing meetings for small or large groups (it has been run effectively for groups of two thousand people before). The originator of Open Space, Harrison Owen, explains that this approach works best when there are the following conditions present: complexity, diversity, conflict, and urgency.

Each meeting has a trained facilitator and a meeting sponsor, but no specific agenda. The meeting sponsor starts the meeting with an overriding 'meeting purpose'. Then the facilitator explains the Open Space process which is essentially about getting everyone to create the agenda themselves and then explore the issues in self-organizing groups. When key issues or aspects of the agenda start to form amongst the different groups, certain people passionate about particular issues come forward as sponsors for different topics. These topics get posted on the meeting bulletin board or digital 'wall' (a shared space or folder for people to access on-line), and the topic sponsors then say a few words about the topic, issue or question of inquiry and people in the wider group choose which topic group they wish to join. People post comments and explorations on the topic wall as the discussions unfold both virtually and in face-to-face groups.

People are free to move between groups cross-pollinating as they go. Each group then collates the key findings and instantly publishes them digitally so everyone can see the findings and go through them as a whole group. Over a matter of a couple of days, all the most important ideas, data, recommendations and questions for further study, along with immediate action plans, are published for all participants and for the entire organization and its wider stakeholders to see. (Note 16)

TIP

HACKATHON

A hackathon is an event format that can help guide organizations and communities toward collective action. It starts with a clearly defined purpose and brief. Participants then self-organize into small teams to brainstorm and prototype new ideas. There are usually mentors who check in throughout the day with the team and guide them forward. The goal is for each team to present their ideas and solutions to a panel of judges, 'dragons' or stakeholders at the end of the event.

Running a hackathon can be great for crowdsourcing and ideation. It is also a great way for nurturing a collaborative and open innovation culture. Participants forge stronger relationships across organizational silos and get an opportunity to connect outside of the traditional organizational roles and responsibilities. Hackathons are very effective at bringing multiple stakeholders into the design process early on, ensuring a variety of parties challenge the design assumptions upfront before too much prototyping of solutions takes place. There is a simple truth that if you are part of designing the solution, you are much less likely to resist the change when it happens.

What is important here is a focused brief supported by pre-event contextual research to avoid getting sidetracked early on in the process. Also of importance is ensuring the right mix of skill types, operative experts and key decision-makers. Throughout the hackathon it is important that the facilitation team record everything that is being discussed. It is their job to capture, collect and then convert the ideas and insights of the hackathon into action and follow up.

A hackathon format that the founder of The Exponentials, Anton Chernikov, has developed called Brainstorm X works like this: the lead facilitator starts the event with a concise presentation, which clearly defines the purpose of the hackathon; participants then break out into pairs to share their stories and initial feedback on the presentation; everyone then gathers into a circle to introduce themselves within the context of the hackathon; what follows is a series of one hour brainstorm sessions around specific pre-prepared questions and challenges; each brainstorm group has a leader who starts by defining the scope of the brainstorm session; the brainstorm leader (preferably part of the overall facilitation team) encourages participants to spend the first 15 minutes of the session asking questions so people understand as much as possible about the challenge before jumping into solution mode. After 40 minutes all the brainstorming groups converge back into the circle to present back key insights. This fast-paced brainstorming approach means that several cycles of ideation and crowdsourcing can happen while groups are mixed up. (Note 17)

TIP

SWARM

Swarm is rather like an in-depth systemic version of a hackathon in that it is a collaborative way of working on complex problems in order to rapidly prototype potential solutions while involving a variety of diverse stakeholders to capture a systemic view. As a formal process it has been originated and developed by a small group of creative social entrepreneurs, through a company called Swarm, to help multiple stakeholders co-create solutions with potential to make a more beautiful world. (Note 18)

Before the actual swarm takes place, a significant amount of effort is undertaken in a 'shaping phase' to explore and articulate the challenge-based problems requiring attention. This can be honed through a series of interviews with a diverse variety of stakeholders, through on-line questionnaires, informal chats, walks, meets and other information gathered.

A group of people who can participate in person for the two to three day swarm are then recruited, ensuring a good balance of dynamics, a range of skills and perspectives, including a number of people with specific prototyping skills useful for the problem being explored, for instance: web coding, service design, business modelling, etc.

Then participants of the swarm receive and digest well-honed briefs on the challenge-based problem along with relevant associated information a few days before the swarm, so they can hit-the-ground-running once the swarm starts.

The swarm is ideally hosted in a place conducive for co-creativity with access to nature where possible. The swarm itself blends creative collaboration, experiential learning and collective intelligence in an open, playful yet vibrant and intensive space.

Participants self-organize into small sub-groups quickly immersing with the problem, accelerating into a 'prototyping phase' with the support of people who can construct, design and shape-up prototypes.

The two to three days are also inter-dispersed with plenty of reflection time, feedback, sharing and inspiration through talks, films and energizers, with emphasis on deep listening, play and fun, as well as time in nature. Wholesome food eaten together and music make up the mix.

The whole swarm experience is often at once uncomfortable, testing and exhilarating as we all embark on our own personal and collective learning journey over this intensive couple of days.

After the swarm, is a 'sense-making phase', where the insights and solutions are gathered and reflected on, fed-back to the attendees and stakeholders, allowing opportunity for further insights, sharing, reflections and builds.

Overall, clients and participants of Swarm have found this process an immensely rich way to solve complex problems rapidly, to gaining a wider lens on the issues they are exploring while developing stronger more autonomous teams and stakeholder relations through the process.

Story Cafés, World Cafés, Open Space Technology, Hackathons, Swarms and other forms of collaboration sessions all aim to bring together, include, engage and empower people in ways that encourage listening, ideating and co-creating in self-organizing ways that transcend traditional hierarchical decision-making processes. This is the life-blood of adaptive, emergent, regenerative business.

Organization specialists Henri Lipmanowicz and Keith McCandless point out that today's operational conventions of agenda-led meetings, presentations, managed discussions, status reports, and such like, are often designed to control and direct rather than to include and engage. Lipmanowicz and McCandless note that introducing tiny shifts in the way people hold meetings, workshops and conversations transforms decision-making in turn unleashing the latent creative potential of people, leading to better decisions, more innovation and more sociality, whereupon we all end up feeling more connected, empowered, responsible and liberated.

With this in mind, they have come up with a menu of 33 well defined yet simple structures that are designed to allow the inclusion of everyone across all levels of the organization and stakeholder community. They refer to these simple structures as

Liberating Structures in their book of the same title. These 33 Liberating Structures range from very simple methods such as Impromptu Networking, Appreciative Interviews and Improv Prototyping, through to more intricate methods such as Ecocycle Planning, Panarchy, Purpose-to-Practice and Wise Crowds. (Note 19)

SYNCHRONICITY

The more we develop our personal and organizational gnosis, the more we will be open to detecting subtly lit pathways amid the fast-changing landscape. Through noticing strong somatic and soulful resonances, repetitive occurrences, coincidences, doors opening, meaningful connections, networks forming with ease, etc. we are able to start making sense of where our emerging future is guiding us.

Richard Barrett views synchronicity as direct promptings from our soul. These soul promptings increase as we learn to activate and deepen our intuition while opening up to more of the underlying inter-relational patterns and rhythms of our given situation. This helps us navigate effectively amid complex fast-moving environments.

Synchronicities more readily occur for us when we are fully attending to the task with passion and purposefulness, ensuring a coherence of head, heart and gut as we fully engage in what we are doing. This coherence is what helps generate a feeling of being in 'flow', as subtly lit paths take us along a flowing route. The hallmark of being in 'flow' is enjoying what we are doing along with a heightened sense of energized focus. The great mythologist Joseph Campbell called this 'finding your bliss' which is a life-learning process of listening to the whispers of the heart with a clear mind and then having the courage to follow our heart's guidance. Cultivating heart-awareness is particularly useful here.

EXAMPLE: Chris Randall, a professional 'flow coach', has worked extensively with Thornton's Budgens, a supermarket in London. Through a number of sessions with senior management and volunteer coaches from different teams across the business, Randall facilitated a process for people to start letting go of previous 'baggage' while starting to open up to what it is they deeply love doing and how they can bring this passion and purpose into daily work activities.

Andrew Thornton, the owner and Chairman of the supermarket, sees this flow work as foundational to enriching the culture of the organization, and providing for: more fulfilled employees, happier customers, more cohesive communities, and greater custodianship and care for the environment. When compared with conventional short-term profit maximization focus, Andrew Thornton has found this flow approach far more sustainable and commercial, helping the supermarket buck the market trend in terms of overall performance. In fact, on the back of this successful initiative Thornton, Randell and others have set up Heart-in-Business Limited to help other organizations become places of passion, authenticity and love *where everyone is doing a job we love doing, where we are all making a difference, we are all heard and understood, and we all hear and understand our colleagues.* (Note 20)

The more our team members and fellow stakeholders develop their personal gnosis, the more the organizational gnosis will collectively form. And likewise, the more our organizational gnosis develops, the easier it is for individuals to 'find their bliss'. It is here, that organizational and personal gnosis start to resonate with each other and extraordinary things begin to spark. This is the sweet spot for our firms of the future to learn to cultivate.

Synchronicities spark up subtly lit pathways for the organization. The wisdom currents flowing through life (Sophia) conspire to help the emergence of our future, as the collective resonance has an effect (either consonance – enhancing, constructing - or dissonance – disrupting, deconstructing) on the deeper fields of resonance within our psychical and physical world.

Learning to tune our resonance both personally and collectively is the artful mastery of journeying toward a firm of the future. What disrupts this resonance is our own ego-awareness attempting to get in the way and dominate things, and likewise the organization's sweet spot starts to get hijacked if we drift back in to the habits of yesterday's logic - short-termism, profit-for-profits sake, 'it's all about the numbers' mentality.

We are not always fully aware of what is going on in the thick of challenging volatile business climes, hence why regular routines, practices and techniques at the personal and organizational level are vital for our journey.

For example, we may be feeling the sweet spot, riding the wave, getting into the flow individually and within our team, and doors are opening for us, deals are happening, clients are connecting, sales converting successfully and projects being delivered synergistically, and we start to get carried away on the wave of this resonance. Rather than checking-in with ourselves and our teams and remaining humble, grounded, receptive and in-tune with the changing ebbs and flows, energies and life-forces, we are naturally excited about our successes and wish to capitalize while times are good.

Hubris can start to creep in, along with a natural desire to grow and extend. Growth and extension are very natural aspects of all living systems, including for our firms of the future, but, as we learn from nature's wisdom, there is a right time for growth and also a right time for reflection and reconfiguration, as much as it may be contrary to our ego-urges. Taking time and space to sense into what stage of the adaptive cycle we are at, what is emerging around and within us personally and organizationally, is wise yet easier said than done in the frenetic thick of it all.

A good metaphor here is of Jazz musicians jamming together, infusing rhythms through group resonance. If one or two musicians get too carried away with their own 'solo' guitar riff or drum fill, then the dynamics of the group and its overall resonance can be affected and the sweet spot lost. Our 'luck' might turn to 'mis-fortune', doors that were opening begin to close or stick ajar, the time is not quite right for that next project, and we must learn to sense this personally and collectively so that we do not force things and so incur expense and resources when the resonance is not there. This is an art. We learn through our mistakes and we get better with practice. Patience is a virtue and the more we learn to sense the flow, pulse and synchronicities of what is unfolding, the more we learn to hold back and be patient, engaging consciously and coherently.

TIP

SOCIAL PRESENCING THEATRE

This is an improvisational embodiment activity where groups of people gently move together while bringing attention to the sensations in our bodies. This art-form or social technology has been co-created by Arawana Hyashi, Otto Scharmer and members of the Presencing Institute and is now being used to great effect in organizations of all shapes and sizes.

Either in pairs or small groups (utilizing the Social Presencing methods of Duets, Village, Field Dance, Stuck Dance, Case-Clinic, Seed Dance and 4-D Mapping) participants move together in improvisational, unplanned, spontaneous ways, or as Otto Scharmer would say, engaging with 'an open mind, open heart and open will'.

Through this practice, we learn to cultivate awareness of our body sensations (our 'somatic awareness') while also sensing the social field we are in as a group while moving together (our 'social awareness'). We simply experience what emerges for us as we explore our movements within this social sphere. This has the immediate impact of cultivating our attention, inner-listening and moment-to-moment mindfulness and general awareness which helps set the right ground work for unlocking fresh ideas, seeing things from a fresh perspective, while letting go of old mind-sets constraining us.

It helps us become more aware of others as we engage our embodied awareness in relation to the movements of others within our group. It helps enhance our connection and inter-dynamics, highlighting motives and needs as well as cultural and unconscious biases. It also helps us cultivate a sense of the social field of our group with any tensions or emotional reactions it may invoke within us.

Once the groups have become comfortable with relaxing into the bodywork and feeling into the gentle movements, the groups can then consciously start to frame certain themes or case-study situations we wish to explore. For instance, how we feel at work in different situations, or envisioning different future scenarios.

This felt experience and group learning affects the participants in subtle yet profound ways, fundamentally changing perspectives and relationship dynamics within teams and across stakeholder groups. It helps foster greater authenticity, connection, receptivity, stillness within movement, systemic awareness, sharing and trust in groups, while allowing the groups to be more open to the generative wisdom of the social field and our individual somatic awareness.

> 'When the body and mind stop fighting or going in different directions, then we can relax and feel less restricted. We appreciate and fully use all our senses. We can accurately perceive whatever situation we find ourselves in. We can pay attention to details and to the whole simultaneously. We develop a panoramic awareness that lessens the sense of separateness between our self and others.'
> *Arawana Hyashi, Presencing Institute* (Note 21)

Through these Social Presencing exercises we directly sense and embody how to open ourselves up to fresh thinking, innovation and co-creativity beyond the abstractions, habituations and ego-chatter of our thinking minds. It helps us shift our awareness from our individual perspectives or 'group-think' patterns into exploring new insights, opening up new fields of exploration while shifting perspectives through what is emerging freshly within the group.

This shift or deepening of our perceptual horizon also assists our general shift from what Otto Scharmer refers to as 'ego to eco', a shift from an 'I' centric perspective to a deeper awareness of the inter-relational ecosystemic nature of our social field; in other words, it helps cultivate a shift from 'yesterday's logic' to a more soulful 'regenerative logic' whereupon we perceive the 'inter-being' of our relations within our teams, wider business context and more-than-human world. Hence plenty of time to debrief after each Social Presencing Theatre session is recommended as it is during these sharing sessions that insights are often revealed, and our felt-sensed experiences and deepening awareness is honored within the team.

These embodied group practices allow participants to develop a felt understanding of Otto Scharmer's Theory U-journey of moving through phases of awareness in order to let-go so as to let-come the emerging future in our organizations. Scharmer's five phases of the U-journey are: co-initiating (tuning into our inner-sense while listening to others around us to sense what life is calling us to do); co-sensing (connecting with others and sensing the emergence within the social field and wider systemic business context); presencing (embracing stillness, being receptive to the generative wisdom, and learning to adapt in open-hearted ways); co-creating (prototyping the future within our teams); co-evolving (embodying the future within our organizations in artful and wise ways that attune with the shifting context). (Note 22)

TIP

APPRECIATIVE INQUIRY

This is a whole-systems approach for organizations that originated out of David Cooperrider's and others' work in the eighties and has since been evolved into different blends. One recent flavour is W-Holistic Appreciative Inquiry, developed by Chris Laszlo and Judy Sorum Brown, which focuses on the whole human being within the frame of systemic transformation. (Note 23)

Fundamentally, Appreciative Inquiry (AI) is a living-systems inquiry approach rooted in positive questioning and collaborative inquiry. It is 'appreciative' in that the line of inquiry is about recognizing the best in people and our context, affirming past and present strengths, successes and potentials, while recognizing the things that enhance our vitality and excellence. It is an 'inquiry' as an act of exploration through questioning in an open, appreciative way.

Through this inquiry we seek new potentials and possibilities. It is a systemic discovery of what gives 'life' to the living system of the organization; an exploration into sharing the stories of when the organization is most alive, most effective and constructive (economically, socially, ecologically). It is the art of asking positive, open questions in a way that reveals the greatest potential of the organization. David Cooperrider provides a couple of framing questions that point to the overall spirit of AI:

'What would happen to our change practices if we began all of our work with the positive presumption that organizations, as centers of human relatedness, are 'alive' with infinite constructive capacity?'

'How can we better inquire into organization existence in ways that are economically, humanly and ecologically significant, that is, in ways that increasingly help people discover, dream, design and transform toward the greatest good?'

There are four stages to AI: Discovery, Dream, Design and Destiny

DISCOVERY is the stage where we gather stories and insights from across the business and wider stakeholder ecosystem. This can be through hundreds of interviews framed through open, positive questions with interviewers who have been trained in the art of AI; this way we start to discover the potential, and art of the possible, within the organization. Here are a couple of example Discovery questions taken from work at GTE, a 67,000 employee telecommunications company: 'Obviously you have had ups and downs in your career at GTE. But for the moment I would like you to focus on a high point, a time in your work experience here where you felt most alive, most engaged, or most successful. Can you tell me the story? How did it unfold? What was it organizationally that made it stand out? What was it about you that made it a high point?'

The act of undertaking these interviews and people sharing positive stories has a transformative effect in its own right. It is 'generative' in that the very undertaking of this intervention helps move people forward, generating the future as we go. As David Cooperrider notes, 'As people throughout a system connect in serious study into qualities, examples, and analysis of the positive core – each appreciating and everyone being appreciated – hope grows and community expands.'

DREAM is the stage where all the insights and stories are gathered together and themes or examples are shared so that we can start to tune into any themes about what makes the organization alive. Areas of visionary propositions are developed and form threads within an interwoven 'convergence zone' forming the 'positive core' of the new dream to be realized by the organization. Again, the undertaking of this process further enhances and enriches collaboration amongst different stakeholders across the organization, who start to develop a widening and deepening awareness of the new world emerging. Then we ask questions about this emerging future, such as: 'What is the world calling us to become? What are those things about us that no matter how much we change, we want to continue into our new and different future?'

Typically about four days of workshops on appreciative analysis, planning and articulation of the different business directions is undertaken; from this, a vision of a better world for the organization, and a powerful purpose and statement of strategic intent forms.

In the **Design** stage we start to plan the redesign of the organization through prototyping and future search planning. A good question to ask here is, 'What would our organization look like if it were designed in every way possible to maximise the qualities of the positive core and enable the accelerated realization of our dreams?' We start rapid prototyping of the new ways, innovating and collaborating as we go and people vote with their feet, joining in on innovations which they are passionate about, prototyping through co-creative processes.

In the **Destiny** stage we focus on how we deepen the chosen prototypes into full scale across the organization, what the implementation plan is, and the governance and task forces needed to make it all happen.

Laszlo and Brown have enriched this AI approach with contemplative and artful activities to ensure personal and organizational gnosis deepens through the process. This is called W-Holistic AI, where additional emphasis is placed on cultivating our soulful awareness within each stage. By example:

DISCOVERY – at the beginning of each interview or group gathering of stories (e.g. Story Café or World Café) a few minutes are dedicated to contemplative presencing, such as conscious breathing and silent reflection. Then the interview or sharing is undertaken with deep listening exercises to deepen the soulfulness of what emerges.

DREAM – We explore our soul-purpose by inquiring into what is our deepest and most profound personal goal of 'what I live for' and then apply what comes from this to the emerging themes and future scenarios we wish to create for our organization.

DESIGN – Expressive artful exercises are undertaken where we express moments of creativity and aliveness in our lives by sharing these experiences through dance or drawing, and then share this in the debrief, and apply this creativity to how we approach the design phase.

DESTINY – Contemplative explorations into how our ways of being need to relate with and enrich our ways of doing in the new world of our organization. We explore what our personal and organizational gnosis 'looks and feels' like, exploring how we maintain this gnosis, what regular practices and artful undertakings, group activities and off-site sessions, etc. we need to factor into our ways of working and governance approaches.

SOULFUL

The soul is the source of our creativity, life-force and deeper life purpose. The more we allow the soul into our awareness, the more authentic we become, the more we feel replenished, replete, alive, and in harmony with what is unfolding in our midst.

The Great Work of our lives is learning to lead and live with this soul-awareness permeating our daily awareness, in-so-doing transforming our beliefs, behaviors, outlook and culture.

It is through this soulful attention that we engage in a loving, heartfelt, embracement of life. We perceive the awe-inspiring beauty of the world around us, and sense the Great Mystery within which we are participating. With this soul-awareness, we enter into the flow of our highest potential, and seek the truth and authenticity within what is unfolding within and all around us. We feel less fearful of change yet also more vulnerable as we are open to life beyond the defensiveness of our ego-barriers, while also feeling more abundant and free to accept what comes our way.

Bringing this soulful way into our busyness requires us to slow down, be patient, receptive and attentive. The leadership specialist Parker J Palmer speaks of the soul being like a wild animal in the woods, and how we easily scare it away with our noisy intrusions and impatient urges. Our challenge as leaders and change agents is to create a working environment and organizational culture that encourages this wild animal into our meetings, conference rooms and corridor discussions.

As we have already discussed, stillness is a powerful way to invite in the soul. We can encourage small mini-moments of stillness into our everyday life: pausing before responding, resisting talking just for the sake of covering over the silence, getting comfortable with long pauses, listening completely without interrupting with our own view, inviting dialogue with others, generating insight, smiling genuinely, looking attentively into the other's eyes, sensing tensions as they arise and being comfortable with holding the tension rather than reacting to it, cultivating an open heart-and-mind attitude, learning not to pre-judge the other but to be open, sensing the wider interconnections, empathizing by putting ourselves in the other's shoes, developing greater capacity for integrating perspectives and differing views, sitting patiently with the uncomfortable feeling of not knowing. As Mother Teresa wisely said, we learn to place small steps with great love.

'The soul is generous: it takes in the needs of the world. The soul is wise, it suffers without shutting down. The soul is hopeful: it engages the world in ways that keep opening our hearts. The soul is creative: it finds a path between realities that might defeat us and fantasies that are mere escapes. All we need to do is to bring down the wall that separates us from our own souls and deprives the world of the soul's regenerative powers.'
Parker J Palmer, leadership specialist

TIP

CIRCLES OF TRUST

Parker J Palmer has provided a detailed study guide in his book *A Hidden Wholeness* on how to best host communities of solitude or 'circles of trust', as places to nurture our soul within groups. Group sizes can vary from around half a dozen to about a dozen people who form a circle. (Note 24) It is preferable if these people are familiar with Way of Council or similar sharing circle practices and so understand the ground rules of speaking and listening from the heart. Parker J Palmer suggests people commit to meeting for one to two hours every week for about ten weeks.

The circle is an invitation to do 'soul work'. We are sharing about the challenges and opportunities going on in our working lives right now for us in a heartfelt and authentic way; sharing our fears and failings as well as our joys and successes with kindred spirits on similar journeys. We learn to cultivate trust in what is emerging within us and the confidence to share it openly in a space free from judgement, interruptions and opinion-forming.

We start and end with a couple of minutes' silence. Stillness is valued throughout the circle, so after someone has spoken we allow a pause to reflect before we jump in with what we wish to share. We do not offer advice to others following what they have shared, we simply listen and where we feel it appropriate we may offer a question to help each other into deeper speech. These questions come from a place of personal motive yet are in service of what is emerging within the circle.

The primacy here is not the content, the 'what', but the 'way', the soulful heartfelt sharing, without specific agendas or outcomes in mind. We are simply creating space to open up and allow the soul to come through. It's simple yet has profound enriching benefits for all involved. As a group we take confidentiality very seriously and what is spoken in the circle stays in the circle.

EXAMPLE: The global pharmaceuticals company, Teva, wished to develop a deeper sense of purpose for its global organization. Rather than using a traditional top-down approach, it sought to get local managers involved in facilitating local workshops around the world. This allowed groups of people to brainstorm what they thought the unique contribution the organization made to the world was for their specific locality. All of the outputs of the workshops were collated and fed into senior managers who embarked on a Wilderness Retreat where they spent 15 hours in silence, by themselves, to ponder on the findings of these workshops in terms of the deeper sense of organizational purpose. After this silent retreat, while still in the wilderness, the executives took part in six rounds of heartfelt discussions over four days to find the common 'soul' of the organization.

Once this soulful sense of purpose was agreed upon, the executives then undertook 'walkabouts' throughout the regions, where they would sit with other executives in a circle, with all the local managers gathered around the circle listening to them share the process they went through in the wilderness, their personal feelings, insights, experiences and how they went about uncovering the organizational sense of purpose. 'Cultural zones' were then set up throughout the global business in coffee areas or meeting areas in different factories and offices throughout the global organization, where notes, pictures, key messages and experiences from all the meetings undertaken, were shared on walls and temporary partitions erected for the zones. Local managers were active in bringing external stakeholders and people across the local business to these zones for coffee breaks and open discussions about Teva's sense of purpose. This is also where local 'gatherings' of one to two hour customized interactive sessions for local people to engage with senior leaders were undertaken so that people were able to ask questions about the sense of purpose and the journey undertaken in finding this purpose.

The soul contains and flows with regenerative wisdom. Its perspective washes away the old belief systems and structures by exposing them for what they are - essentially ego-based, fear-based, control-based limitations stifling our deeper humanity. The Social Darwinist worldview that permeates much of our business behavior (dog-eat-dog competition, dominate or be dominated, selfish self-agency wins the struggle for survival) begins to dissolve as a more collaborative, participatory worldview of inter-being flows more freely in our conscious awareness. (Note 25) As a groundswell of decision-makers and stakeholders cultivate this soulful way, the organization begins to cross the threshold from the firm of the past to the firm of the future, and no longer does the ethos of 'short-term profit maximization for the few at the expense of the many' hold water.

Let's take a moment to ask ourselves these questions:

Why are we here doing what we are doing?

What are we in business for – what is the real underlying purpose?

What value are we delivering to society? What about to the wider fabric of life?

Do we wish our activities to help or hinder life?

This personal and organizational shift from yesterday's logic to a more soulful way is fraught with psychological trip wires, cognitive cul-de-sacs and cultural barriers. It asks us to dig deep and have courage as we nurture the metamorphosis of our consciousness, allowing the soul to pervade more and more of how we act and interact.

THE ARTFUL ORGANIZATION

Expressive arts have been successfully used in business for some years now; in fact the majority of Fortune 500 companies are actually already using various art forms as part of organizational development activities. Through interactive, improvised and reflective artful undertakings (photography, storytelling, dancing, drawing, visualizing, singing, journaling, poetry, collages, sculpting, and such like) individuals and teams of people can get involved in an active and transformative process that takes us deeper into ourselves. (Note 26)

Artful undertakings can help us open up to and challenge assumptions that may be holding us back, and help us express concerns, fears and anxieties in times of change, unshackling ourselves from the grasping grip of our ego-personas. This helps cultivate our other ways of knowing beyond that of our rationalizing thinking-head as we explore ways to express our feelings, emotions and felt-senses informed by our somatic awareness, intuitions and 'unconscious' perturbations and resonances.

> 'Artistic skill is the combining of many levels of mind
> – unconscious, conscious and external – to make a
> statement of their combination.'
> *Gregory Bateson, cyberneticist and social ecologist*

These artful undertakings are a powerful way for us to get comfortable with exploring more of ourselves within our workplaces while in the company of our colleagues and wider stakeholder communities. They can help us shift out-dated modes of thinking, challenge cultural dynamics, assumptions and group-think which hold us back from exploring, igniting and embodying our deeper sense of purpose at personal and organizational levels. We learn to open up to our uncertainty and engage in rich experiential aliveness with our colleagues, sensing first-hand how to experience 'flow' within our teams.

Such artful practices can explore specific themes that need addressing, they can also act as one-off disruptions as part of a transformational project or as part of a specific creative process (helping us move more fluently from open and closed states of mind while working on innovative ventures), or as part of enhancing team dynamics and organizational culture. In this respect, they can be used with a specific problem, situation and goal in mind. However, they can also be enfolded into the very way in which an organization operates on a daily basis, 'embedded into the DNA' of the organization.

Regular interventions of artful expressions help us share our own tensions, fears, vulnerability, experiences and learnings that are hidden within us beyond verbalization and brainstorming. Freud, then Jung, and now James Hillman, as well as other great psychologists, have discovered that the psyche is imaginal and by relating with the images that come up through our unconscious into our conscious mind through artful undertakings - such as dance, drawing or sculpting - we can get closer to interpreting the image, feeling its insight within us and so opening up to this expression emanating from what we have experienced yet cannot rationalize. We allow more of ourselves to come through and inform our ways of being and doing, in the process enriching our ability to innovate, adapt and evolve amid volatile times.

Many of us have come across organizations that have had the courage and insight to host creative interventions or workshops as one-off or yearly affairs, yet not so common are the organizations that recognize the importance of embedding this artful way of knowing into the daily, weekly and monthly rhythm of operations. A firm of the future is a truly artful organization where artful expression, provocation and exploration become part of the cultural way of being and doing.

Space and time is allocated on a regular basis for artful embodiment to take place individually, within workgroups, and diverse stakeholder groups spanning different geographies. Through these artful undertakings we allow for a continual tuning-in to what we need to let go of, give space to, experience, and learn from, while embracing our emerging future. We continuously maintain a rich gnosis through a broad and deep 'epistemological horizon'. This is exactly what we need in order to successfully deal with unceasing transformation within our personal, organizational and systemic context.

This embedding of artful knowing into the daily rhythms of the organization ensures our personal and organizational gnosis is kept alive as part-and-parcel of our evolving organizational culture. Therefore the artful firm of the future ensures its sense of purpose is continually revisited and keep alive, while our conversations, team dynamics, projects, and creative endeavors are all kept flowing in an artful way. Becoming artful is essentially about becoming more fully human in a firm of the future, because each and every one of us are artists engaging in the artful endeavour of life lived in a soulful, expressive and authentic way.

'Every human being is an artist, a freedom being called to participate in transforming and reshaping the conditions, thinking and structures that shape and inform our lives.'
Joseph Beuys, artist

Dr Chris Seeley and Ellen Thornhill of Ashridge Business School published an insightful report entitled *Artful Organization* in March 2014. In this, a four-step approach for artful knowing in organizations is put forward:

1.   SENSUOUS ENCOUNTERING – we begin our artful undertaking by becoming aware of our somatic response to aesthetic experiences such as colour, taste, music, dancing. We open up to our senses and bring our bodily reactions and responses into our conscious awareness.

2.   SUSPENDING – we then hang fire before we attempt to respond with our thinking mind. The temptation with any disruption is to jump in with a quick head-response as we do not like the ambiguity the disruption presents. Here, we are learning to cultivate our tolerance of this uncomfortable ambiguity and mild anxiety related to 'not knowing', holding ourselves back from prematurely ejaculating a half-baked response (recall John Cleese's insights discussed earlier, that learning to hold back and stay in the 'open mode' for longer heightens our creativity ensuring richer outcomes). This is an opportunity for us to expand our receptivity prior to responding, opening ourselves up to receiving inspiration from our deeper ways of knowing while paying attention to our bodily sensations and perturbations.

3.   BODYING-FORTH – allowing impulses and non-verbal tacit knowings within us to be expressed through the

expressive arts channel of choice whether that be improvisational acting, dancing, singing, drawing, sculpting clay, and such like. Being messy, not worrying about the outcome and not being ego-attached to what we body-forth, we openly let go and just play with what emerges in a vulnerable, generative and exploratory way. This can be done individually or in pairs and groups. For instance, Social Presencing Theatre, Applied Improvisation, Interplay, Sociodrama, Action Methods and Constellations are all well-versed ways of engaging in facilitated group expressions. (Note 27)

4. **BEING IN-FORMED** – After spending time on the above stages, we allow for an enriching exploration within us and within our teams to occur, whereupon we give space and energy to what really wants to come through us, allowing our ways of knowing beyond the rationalizing mind to have their say. This allows for a deeper soul-infused wisdom to emerge and inform the transformation we are working through. This can then form part of on-going action research and collective inquiry within our teams as we go about our daily business amid unceasing transformation.

By embedding this artful knowing into our regular working life, we are allowing our everyday work to become a lived artful experience which is, after all, what life ought to be. And importantly, we are allowing our organization to have the inbuilt creativity and freshness to emerge and evolve as a living, soulful enterprise.

EXAMPLE: Since 2009, Daniel Ludevig as Director of MOVE Leadership, has been exploring the potential of embodied knowledge to enhance leaders, teams and organizations. (Note 28)

Applying cutting-edge artful undertakings – movement exercise, dance, improvisation, body sculptures and Social Presencing Theatre along with a variety of other creative-based methodologies – Ludevig has helped a wide range of large and small businesses deal with transformational change while helping people explore conscious and unconscious perceptions and biases, deeper ways of knowing, relationship connections and leadership preferences. These artful, embodied expressions allow for tangible, lively facilitated experiences where we directly perceive change-invoked challenges within ourselves and our groups. In a playful, high-energy, mindful and fun way, we gain direct experience of our own prejudices, emotions, aversions, cultural and unconscious biases, and judgements that get in the way of our ability to open up and explore challenges with a fresh, creative perspective.

After each movement exercise lots of time is given for facilitated verbal debrief, sharing and exploration. It is here that direct application to daily work-life can be revealed within teams. These debriefs are usually full of laughter and encourage open sharing in a deep way because we have all shared in the creative art-based experience together and had first-hand embodied practical knowledge as a felt-sense which provokes our insights, learning and sharing. This helps us get 'comfortable with the uncomfortable' within our own selves and within the dynamics of the team. Quite quickly, the real issues of what is worrying us or holding us back start to emerge.

At a leading European banking institution, Ludevig was asked to work with senior leadership teams who were experiencing tensions amid significant change in the organization. Despite resistance and hesitation to begin with, an initial two-day interactive session proved to be a turning point in bringing the entire team together from a place of political infighting to deep sharing, honesty, openness and empathy which unlocked innovation and creativity while rebuilding trust. With this openness and willingness to move forward, the team engaged in sculpture building to help visualize various scenarios for their strategic planning. Following the success of this initial intervention, Ludevig has undertaken regular sessions every six months over the last three years with the bank, applying movement and creative-based approaches to help address difficult challenges needing to be worked through. Over this time, the team has developed a deeper level of connection, trust, openness and alignment on values and approaches to value-creation.

By way of summarizing this module on organizational gnosis and also relating it with the other modules covered so far, we shall revisit Richard Barrett's seven stages of personal psychological develop and map them to seven stages of organizational development, illustrating our journey toward a firm of the future. [Note 29]

LEVELS OF CONSCIOUSNESS	ORGANIZATION ACTIONS AND NEEDS	DEVELOPMENTAL TASKS
1 - Surviving	Creating: Forming a financially independent, profitable entity while ensuring the general welfare of the core stakeholder community.	Surviving: Becoming a viable organizational entity with clear value propositions and a viable business model with operational values in place.
2 - Relating	Learning: Learning to deal with conflicts, tensions and multi-stakeholder dynamics while fostering a sense of trust, integrity, belonging and loyalty across the core stakeholder community.	Harmonizing: Creating and nurturing a conscious culture that seeks to strive toward personal and organizational gnosis through mutual respect, openness, authenticity, diversity and collaboration.
3 - Differentiating	Establishing: Developing policies, procedures, practices, principles and processes that allow for high performing values-based teams to flourish in challenging fast-evolving situations.	Performing: Efficient and effective running of the day-to-day operations while bringing in deeper values, measures and behaviors beyond short-term financial metrics.
4 – Transformation	Transforming the organization: through both incremental and radical innovations that allow for adaptive cycles of continuous change to be embedded at nested levels throughout the organization.	Empowering: Enabling employees to take greater responsibility, autonomy and active participation in innovating and co-creating new ways of operating and organizing.

5 - Internal Cohesion	Aligning motivations: forming a soul-based vision and aligning employee motivations around a shared set of values and behaviors. Embedding the core ways of being and doing into the organizational culture. Living the motto 'small steps with great love'.	Bonding: Working on the internal cohesion of a high-trust soul-based culture so that our personal gnosis and organizational gnosis start to mutually reinforce each other.
6 – Making a Difference	Enhancing resilience: synergizing across boundaries, nurturing vibrant reciprocity across the business ecosystem (social, ecological, economic).	Collaborating: Deepening our communication approaches, values and value-based reciprocity with a diverse ecosystem of stakeholders both locally and globally.
7 - Service	Deepening the gnosis: strategic and operational vision, methods and mind-set aligned toward regenerative business.	Serving: Serving the fabric of life, creating net-positive value for both human and more-than-human stakeholders.

As we progress along our journey toward becoming a firm of the future, we transcend and include each level of consciousness, till the organization starts to operate at what Barrett refers to as 'full spectrum' consciousness where all stages are evident within the psyche and culture of the organization.

I have yet to come across an organization operating at this 'full spectrum' consciousness, but there are plenty of examples of organizations actively developing their organizational gnosis as they journey toward becoming future-fit, many of which have been mentioned in these pages (Thornton's Budgens, Whole Foods, Zappos, Buurtzorg, Menlo Investments, FAVI, Triodos, Scott Bader, Sounds True and Interface, for instance). In a recent interview I conducted with the world-renowned systems-theorist, Fritjof Capra, I asked if he had examples of organizations embracing living systems logic, and he offered these: Gore & Associates (manufacturers of Gore-Tex), Ideo (a design company in San Francisco), Vagas (a Brazilian employment agency), Impact Hub (a global network of social-enterprise community centers), Zentrum für Integrale Führung (a consulting group in Austria), and Amana-Key (a consulting group in Brazil). [Note 30] And there are, no doubt, lots of other interesting cases the world over to provide insight for our own organizations whatever the size and sector.

REFLECTIVE QUESTIONS

Looking at the seven levels of organizational consciousness table, at what level would you put your organization?

Is there a reality-gap between the values your organization espouses and day-to-day work-life?

How can you improve your organization's gnosis through your own sphere of influence?

Can you think of some small steps you can take to change communications and meeting conventions in a way that encourage more collaboration and self-organization?

How can you transform your weekly schedule to give more space and time for sharing in soulful ways with your team, to invite in soulful conversations, and to start exploring new ways of operating and organizing?

What would it take for you to help organize and support a soul circle for team members to sit and share in confidence once a fortnight?

If you were tasked with making the business case for your organization committing to becoming a firm of the future, what would you include in the business case and who would you engage across the business and stakeholder community to help you?

MODULE **SIX**

LEADING ACROSS THE THRESHOLD

AMID INCREASING COMPLEXITY, THE
JOURNEY TOWARD A FIRM OF THE
FUTURE REQUIRES MULTIPLE THRESHOLDS
TO BE CROSSED, ASKING EACH OF US
TO BE CONSCIOUS, COURAGEOUS AND
COMPASSIONATE LEADERS, LEADING
FROM OUR HEART WHILE USING
OUR HEAD.

EXECUTIVE SUMMARY

- As leaders, we first embark on our own personal gnosis. As we develop our own self-mastery, we are better able to lead, coach and guide others.

- Five important areas for our firm of the future leaders to focus on in their organizations are: communication; innovation; diversity; sense of purpose; time and space.

- Five qualities for conscious leadership are: waking up; self-mastery; relating and collaborating; working effectively with millennials; and synchronicity.

- Effective leaders work from the deepest levels of their being and are courageous in leading from the heart with a coherent ego-soul dynamic; they are listeners, coaches, facilitators and catalysts who are continually attuning the yin-yang qualities within themselves and their work environments.

'THE MOST EXCITING BREAKTHROUGHS
OF THE 21ST CENTURY WILL NOT OCCUR
BECAUSE OF TECHNOLOGY, BUT
BECAUSE OF AN EXPANDING CONCEPT
OF WHAT IT MEANS TO BE HUMAN.'
JOHN NAISBITT, FUTURIST

THE ALREADY DISTANT MEMORY OF the year 2014 has been dubbed the 'great wake up', a harbinger for what lies ahead, a proliferation of 'non-normative' strategic ruptures to the interwoven socio-economic, corporate and political global operating system: Ebola devastation in West Africa, Islamic State (IS), the refugee crisis, Sony's cyber-attacks, Volkswagen's expose, Greece's looming debt crisis, sovereign debt mountains the world over, the Ukraine crisis, Brazil's and Russia's economic woes, and China's economic slowdown, are just some of the contributors to 2014's great wake-up call that the world is not going to simply return to business-as-usual. As Director of the Institute of Statecraft, Chris Donnelly, has said, the rate of change we are now going through is comparable to what happens in war time.

In an interim report for the Churchill 2015 21st Century Statesmanship Global Leaders Programme, Nik Gowing and Chris Langdon explore the new imperative for leadership in these transformational times. [Note 1] Sixty confidential in-depth interviews at the highest level across business and government show an 'executive myopia': short-termism, risk aversion and systemic fear, internalized focus on cost-cutting rather than out-of-the-box thinking, cognitive overload and dissonance, top-level reluctance blended with anxiety, frailties and fatigue. Whilst this report is UK-focused, it compliments other reports from other parts of the world and contributes to a rich-picture forming of a systemic 'complexity gap' in leadership across the globe.

This is not to undermine a number of positive developments taking place on complex global leadership issues such as the UN Global Goals campaign and the COP21 agreements in Paris in late 2015, where a variety of non-political stakeholders in business and beyond helped secure a constructive outcome. Yet, the cold reality is the majority of our leaders – across government, corporations and non-profit institutions – are struggling to cope with the current conditions. And things are only set to get yet more complex, uncertain and challenging.

Gowing and Langdon ask the important and timely question facing many of today's leaders, 'how to break the arm lock created by the cost of challenging conformity and risk aversion at a time when the need for speed and agility is paramount?' [Note 2] Unilever's CEO, Paul Polman, speaks to this by saying that first and foremost a leader must find their inner compass. It is this inner compass that guides us in these turbulent times while pulling us beyond threat rigidity, risk aversion, group think and short-termism into deeper systems-intelligence.

CEO of Whole Foods, John Mackey, and co-founder of Conscious Capitalism Raj Sisodia refer to this deeper systems-intelligence as spawning from a coherence of IQ, EQ and SQ, whereupon as leaders we begin to 'systems-feel' through the complexity with heightened intuitive awareness and inner-clarity, at once being more humble, empathic, authentic and receptive to internal and external feedback, able to say 'I don't know' while working with others to explore our emerging future. [Note 3]

Here are five important areas for leaders to focus on in these transformational times:

COMMUNICATION: to commune with others, really listen and share with our peers and stakeholders within and beyond the organization by creating collaborative networks that do more than just brainstorm by having the remit to prototype the future.

INNOVATION: within the organization 'accelerator skunkworks', 'incubators' or 'innovation hubs' operate like cocoons in stealth mode (Google X, for instance) where bright out-of-the-box innovators across the organization can engage in entrepreneurial explorations, with the support of the organization to invest in these prototypes, testing them out before the activities are either spun off or integrated into the main business.

DIVERSITY IN THE BOARDROOM: yes we need more diversity and inclusiveness in terms of age, sex and race, yet also in our ways of thinking, by bringing in non-conformists that provoke and cajole with different perspectives and insights. This can be achieved through inviting a wider range of Non-executive Directors, having a greater variety of external advisers, and utilizing innovative forward-thinking consultants beyond the traditional mainstream consultancies.

SENSE OF PURPOSE: As Polman notes, we need to cultivate our inner-compass, develop our own coherence within ourselves, taking time and energy to embark on a process of 'knowing thy self' so as to understand our deeper sense of purpose beyond our ego-personas and acculturated masks. When we align our outer actions with our inner sense of purpose we allow a deeper creative impulse and authenticity to flow through our work. Ditto for our teams and stakeholders.

TIME AND SPACE: taking personal responsibility for our work schedules and recognizing that the continual busyness and stress actually undermines our ability to think out-of-the-box and sense our inner compass. Each of us can be more effective at managing our diaries, creating blocks in our schedule for 'systemic thinking' where we can reflect, pause and learn to tune-in to our more intuitive awareness and authentic, soulful selves.

There is no sustainable transformation without leadership. It is leadership that gets us to traverse our own thresholds and to help others traverse theirs. The root of the word leadership is *leith* which means 'to go forth and cross the threshold', to let go of old ways while allowing new ways to take root.

As leaders, we first embark on our own personal gnosis. We are pioneers in our own journey, forming experiences and insights that we can share with our fellow team players and stakeholder community. And as we develop our own self-mastery, we are better able to lead, coach and guide others. As Mac Macartney notes, 'A leader is anyone who in whatever capacity emboldens others to live their life with courage, hope, and integrity. Such leaders embody qualities that inspire others to their own journey of authenticity and service.' [Note 4] To be a leader in this capacity requires that we master our own ego-soul dynamic, and so are able to call upon the deeper aspects of our being amid varied and challenging situations, in-so-doing provoking and calling into action deeper aspects within others. It is this kind of authentic leadership that our organizations desperately need.

In Scilla Elworthy's rich and far-ranging work in dealing with conflict transformation, reconciliation and global leadership, she has worked with a variety of top leaders across business, politics, communities and grass-roots activism. [Note 5] The number one most important requirement she has consistently found essential for effective leadership is a shift in personal consciousness. By developing our own self-awareness and cultivating our personal gnosis, we awaken our own energetic potential which flows through our communications, relations and activities.

Being an effective leader in these transformative times is less about what we are doing and more about the way we are being. For Nan Huai Chin, a Zen Buddhist and Taoist Master, the seven steps toward being a great leader are actually seven places of being: awareness, stopping, calmness, stillness, peace, true thinking, attainment. [Note 6] Bringing awareness into what is happening, and pausing (or as Nan Huai Chin says 'stopping') before we react is fundamental to our starting to transcend old habitual responses and patterns of behavior. This is not as easy as it sounds, because it is ingrained in us to react quickly, to be seen to be in control, to be seen to have the answers and be quick to action in vulnerable challenging moments. Yet, we actually need to cultivate the awareness and courage to stay in our vulnerability for a moment or two, to hold back on our reaction and sense into what is really required beyond conditioned responses. This is the first and most fundamental step toward cultivating our gnosis in the midst of stressful challenging environments. It is within the space we create amid the moments and movements of our daily work schedules that we allow our deeper ways of knowing to cohere within us.

> 'The first step toward effective action is nonaction: the ability to avoid the all-too-common impulse to leap into action when an adaptive challenge rears its head...This is not easy in today's fast-food, hurry-up-and-get-on-with-it-world. But it is essential.'
> *Ronald Heifetz, Alexander Grashow, Marty Linsky, leadership specialists* [Note 7]

Awareness is our ability to sense the here-and-now unencumbered by a dominating ego-logic. Rather than reacting, we sense into the situation, and become receptive. Our responsiveness is then informed by this receptivity rather than our impatient impulses. By allowing a deeper coherence of our ways of knowing to be held within us we cultivate the art of becoming a conscious leader through the dynamic of receptive-responsive-reciprocity.

Co-founder of the Global Centre for Conscious Leadership, Gina Hayden, has identified five main qualities or themes that are fundamental for conscious leadership in the times we now live in: waking up; self-mastery; relating and collaborating; working effectively with millennials; and synchronicity. (Note 8) The first two of these relate to our personal gnosis, or to use Hayden's phrase, the 'I' dimension, the third and fourth relate to organizational gnosis, or the 'we' dimension, and the fifth relates to a systemic worldview shift, or the 'it' dimension. Let's explore each of these:

1. **WAKING UP:** The initial step to becoming a conscious leader is our waking up to who we are beyond the constructs, personas and masks of our ego-self. It is in this waking up process that we start to become conscious of the ego-soul dynamic Richard Barrett refers to. According to Hayden's research, this waking up is a deep knowing that emerges within us either as a 'lightning bolt' or a 'gradual sunrise'.

   The lightning bolt wake-up is sudden, provoked by a certain life event, peak experience or personal rupture that shifts our perceptual framing to such an extent that it forces us to see outside our narrow ego-self for more than the briefest of moments.

   The gradual sunrise wake-up is a slower more progressive opening up to who we are while letting go of the strangle-hold of our ego-masks and ingrained behaviors. This may well involve bouts of depression, periods of soul-searching, and deep questioning of our current life style, relationships, work-life and values, along with a mid-life crisis or 'dark night of the soul' which may span many months or years.

2. **SELF-MASTERY:** On the back of this 'waking up', we start to transform our lives, our daily habits and routines, our ways of relating with others and the values we wish to adhere to, while actively working on 'who' and 'how' we are being in the world. Making mistakes, tripping over ourselves, reflecting and learning as we go, we begin to embody what works well for us. We learn to recognize when we are being more graceful and authentic, and when we are getting caught up in our ego-chatter, fears, projections and habits of old. This all comes with an increasing felt-sense of deeply knowing what feels right and what does not as we begin to attune our values and behaviors while learning to be more authentic, more our 'real selves' as our deeper soulful nature starts to shine through. This also comes with a more abundant mind-set where our general outlook is to have faith and trust in what is emerging, not holding too tightly to pre-defined outcomes or expectations, instead trusting that what develops will provide rich learning for us.

   An attitude of gratitude starts to pervade our daily consciousness along with a more relative and systemic perspective about how things are, rather than a black-or-white set of opinions and pre-judgements. This all develops hand-in-hand with a deeper recognition of our self-responsibility and self-determination to cultivate a daily, weekly and monthly routine which makes time and space for reflection, mindfulness, rejuvenation, play-time, inspiration and companionship. We start to cultivate our own way of living authentically.

3. **RELATING AND COLLABORATING:** As we shift our perspective from black-and-white thinking to a more relational and systemic perspective, we value the validity

of multiple viewpoints and diverse discussions, and we learn to appreciate that in our team discussions there are no right answers *per se*, only opportunities for constructive explorations that enrich the parties involved, sparking innovation through collaboration. So, our effectiveness as conscious leaders is essentially about creating the right conditions, dynamics and space for these constructive explorations to form and unfold.

Learning to listen to what is bubbling up in the organization and wider business context comes with a shift in seeing the organization as a living regenerative system inter-related with other living systems at nested levels. What allows for these living systems to thrive is healthy self-organizing, collaborating dynamics of purposeful people co-creating systemic value. Therefore, the conscious leader embraces a fundamental shift in power dynamics from control, hierarchy, ownership, competition and power-over others, to empowering others through generative discussions, listening, sharing and convening space for collaboration to flourish in emergent, self-organizing ways. This is essentially about creating environments where people feel safe in bringing their whole selves to work, to embrace all of their ways of knowing and to openly explore their own ego-soul dynamic in the work-place.

Fritjof Capra notes that a fundamental aspect of all living systems is the emergence of novelty through creativity. Therefore, for an organization to become a thriving living system, our leaders needs to facilitate the emergence of novelty and creativity through building and nurturing a questioning, experimenting, exploring, and learning culture. He notes that, 'Emergence requires an active network of communications. Facilitating emergence, therefore, means first of all building up and nurturing such networks of communications, and creating a learning-culture in which continual questioning is encouraged and innovation is rewarded. The experience of the critical instability that precedes the emergence of novelty may involve uncertainty, fear, confusion, or self-doubt. Experienced leaders recognize these emotions as integral parts of the whole dynamics and create a climate of trust and mutual support. During the change process some of the old structures may fall apart, but if the supportive climate and the feedback loops in the network of communications persist, new and more meaningful structures are likely to emerge. When that happens, people often feel a sense of wonder and elation, and now the leader's role is to acknowledge these emotions and provide opportunities for celebration.' (Note 9)

4. **LEADING IN THE MILLENNIAL AGE:** There are lots of sweeping generalizations flying about these days regarding millennials. Hayden sums it up well when she notes that there are conscious 'awake' millennials who really 'get it', who are natural systemic thinkers passionate about making a more vibrant, flourishing future possible, and there are plenty of 'asleep' or 'unconscious' millennials who are simply too caught up in the techno-sphere, paralysis of choice, ego-security, traditional career paths, and the consumer culture, to feel the need to contribute to radical systemic change through their work.

The 'awake' millennials naturally sense the deeper inter-relational nature of our world and the complexity of the challenges we now face. They are passionate about purposeful work and constantly need reassurance and feedback that their work is relevant and of significance in contributing to this Great Transition. Hence, conscious leaders need to be available and responsive enough to provide this constant feedback in order to keep these millennials inspired and buoyed as they go about doing passionate work in unconventional 'out-of-the-box' ways.

As leaders we can use our understanding of the prevalent power structures, hierarchies and yesterday's logic to work with the current system in order to create space beyond the confines and burdens of this system for millennials to bring their whole selves to work in passionate and purposeful ways. We learn to let go of defined ways of doing things and learn to be open to ideas coming from anywhere within and beyond the organization while being conscious of the multiple points of feedback that need our attention and guidance. The essential question to ask ourselves here is, 'how do I help people achieve their own significance?' (Note 10)

5. SYNCHRONICITY: As we foster more emergent, self-organizing and soulful ways of working, a deeper realization that the world is essentially synchronistic is allowed to emerge in our teams. This is a profound worldview shift from the old logic of hyper-competition, domination and separation to a deep felt-knowing that the world is an inter-connected field of relational emergence that we are all co-participating in; a knowing that our intention and attention affects the inter-connections we co-create.

The quality of our awareness is what allows pathways to light up, connections to happen, doors to open, trust to be formed. This deep shift in worldview helps us transcend paradoxes in times of crises, sense pathways amid increasing complexity, and presence emerging futures in fast-changing diverse fields of possibilities. [Note 11] With this deeply embodied synchronistic belief, we recognize how our personal, organizational and systemic activities benefit the whole. Every interaction contributes and has knock-on effects at nested levels, and so the humbling importance of placing conscious steps of change which heal and help rather than exploit and undermine. Through this synchronistic worldview the only real option available to us is to be regenerative.

Business coach, BT Global Challenge round-the-world yacht skipper and Polar Race participant Manley Hopkinson speaks of 'compassionate leadership' as essential for dealing with these emergent and transformative dynamics. [Note 12] For Hopkinson, compassionate leadership is having the consciousness to see the other person, beyond ego filters and judgements, to understand their needs and contextual situation, and therefore help them cross their own thresholds with compassion. His Big Five values for attaining compassionate leadership are:

1. AWARENESS – through 'knowing thy self' we cultivate an awareness that understands the team and the wider business context.

2. COURAGE – A continual commitment to opening up to life as a learning process of becoming our authentic selves: our life journey.

3. CONFIDENCE – Each of us having the belief and conviction in ourselves to cross thresholds, to let go of certainty and enter unchartered waters, determined to succeed through adherence to practice and patience.

4. JOY – Recognizing the innate beauty of life, the clarity and aliveness of the here-and-now, and reminding ourselves of this joy as often as possible.

5. COMPASSION – Acting with heartfelt intent on the needs of others gleaned through our empathic insight - our ability to truly see others as they are.

Hence, compassionate leadership becomes a way of living our lives, a continuous inquiry, an unfolding process of becoming true to our nature. Hopkinson notes that 'conscious communication' is vital to all of this. By conscious communication Hopkinson means soul-to-soul dialogue, where we spend time to develop meaningful relationships with our team members and stakeholder communities so that we relate as engaged learners, gaining insights from our shared perspectives. His research has found the following aspects foundational to conscious communication:

- Listening

- Questioning

- Developing empathy/rapport

- Giving feedback

- Coaching

- Story telling (Note 13)

We have touched on much of this already, but it is worth re-clarifying each of these important points here before we move on:

LISTENING – active and deep listening is when we give our full attention to the conversation, becoming aware of not just the words but of the feeling being conveyed and also any non-verbal cues, such as body gestures, facial expressions, tone of voice and also what is arising in ourselves as gut feelings, intuitive senses of rising emotions, and such like. Psychology professor Albert Mehrabian's research shows that much of what we communicate is non-verbal with on average 55% of our communication coming from the body, 38% coming from sound and tones, and only 7% coming from the actual words. A compassionate leader learns to tune-in to everything, verbal and non-verbal, sensing into what is being conveyed with receptivity in order to reflect and respond wisely.

> 'Great leaders have always been great listeners.'
> *Richard Branson, founder of Virgin*

QUESTIONING – There are a variety of different ways to pose questions with our non-verbal cues and conscious intent influencing the 'way' the question lands for the recipient. Essentially, we keep our questions short, free from prejudices and ensure our attitude is one of exploration, of wishing to learn, not to judge or impatiently jump to pre-defined opinions or desired outcomes. Questioning also utilizes our skill of listening actively and deeply.

DEVELOPING EMPATHY – By opening ourselves up to 'what is' and letting go of ego-chatter and ego-judgments, we allow ourselves to be more receptive to what the other person is sharing with us. Also, through cultivating heart-awareness, we can enhance our capacity to put ourselves in the other's shoes and sense different perspectives beyond our own.

GIVING FEEDBACK – We are social, loving, sharing creatures, so the more we can share with others and give feedback in constructive ways the more we strengthen our social relations and enhance our learning as well as other's learning. Giving feedback is a reciprocal sharing both ways; as we offer feedback we should also be attentive to what emerges within the reciprocity of the sharing itself.

COACHING – The art of effective coaching is a book in itself, and there are many good books on this. Essentially, coaching in this context means perceiving our conversations as reciprocal learning explorations. As Hopkinson notes, coaching is flexible, non-judgemental and enabling, not prescriptive or instructional. It is a two-way process of development, and different from consulting which is advisory.

STORYTELLING – Sharing stories gets people interested, and inspires them in a different way than telling people what to do or instructing them. Story-telling appeals to our left and right brain hemisphere of our head as well as our heart and gut, whereas instructional commands speak largely from and to the left brain hemisphere.

TIP

ART OF HOSTING

The Art of Hosting is a powerful approach for leading in complex and challenging situations. It suggests that those leaders who are able to listen to and draw upon different perspectives, and to strengthen connections between people and organizations through dialogue, will be able to bring out the

best in those whom they are leading. James Allen, of
Sustainability Labs in Brazil, has been involved with the Art of
Hosting (AoH) network. He shares with us here his experience
of this art of hosting as a powerful approach to leadership. (Note 14)

Brazil's 14th AoH get-together was a five-day long meeting, set
in beautiful woodlands not far from Sao Paulo in early 2013. It
is called an 'encounter', rather than a course, because learning
takes place through active participation in a sequence of
workshops that draw on different group dynamics, such as
World Café and Collective Story Harvesting. Participants are
encouraged to take the reins and lead different exercises, with
the aim of drawing on and harvesting collective intelligence, i.e.
the knowledge and wisdom of the whole group, rather than a
chain of individual perspectives.

In this way, participants act as volunteer facilitators, responsible
for leading each session, with the aim of 'hosting and harvesting
meaningful conversations'. For a conversation to be meaningful,
participants must seek to listen actively and speak with intent.
As such, the starting point is the individual's relationship with
themselves. Silence and meditation techniques form part of the
AoH toolkit, since the ability to listen well, both to yourself and
to others, is a *sine qua non* of good leadership.

The relationship between the individual and the others within
the group is first established through the most ancient form of
dialogue, the circle. In the center of the circle, rather than a fire,
is the group's 'purpose', the issue or question that the collective is
burning to address. Much time is spent on the wording and
structure of that question so that the conversations and debates
that follow are coherent and meaningful. Here the host plays an
important role in helping to shape a powerful question, one that
is both inspirational and practical.

What often follows in many of the participatory technologies shared in AoH are break-out groups of between four and six people. A group with that number of participants is large enough and sufficiently diverse to draw on a multitude of perspectives, without being so big that it becomes unwieldy. It is a model that reflects what is happening in many leading companies where self-organizing pods or cells are formed in order to deliver specific processes or results: Google ('projects always start with a small group of people that make traction' says Larry Page) and Kyocera's Amoeba management system are two such examples.

Disagreement within these groups is seen as healthy, indeed is actively encouraged. As management guru Peter Drucker is quoted as saying, the best decisions are based 'on the clash of conflicting views, the dialogue between different points of view, the choice between different judgments. The first rule in decision-making is that one does not make a decision unless there is disagreement.' In fact, conclusions and good decisions ('convergence') can and should only occur after 'divergence' or discordance, where doubts are addressed through pertinent questioning. A good host knows how to needle and question, and embraces difference as part of a collective decision making process.

As such, to lead in this context means to accept the chaos that arises when different people bring their opinions to the table. At its purest form, a collective decision making process can be almost anarchic, in which the group or groups organize themselves and people fit in and contribute in the way they best see fit. Physicist David Bohm's Theory of Dialogue proposes that a meaningful dialogue of enquiry should have no rules, no agenda, and the participants should not be chosen but should put themselves forward. Many of these ideas permeate the AoH encounters: the 'Law of Two Feet' for example says that if 'at any moment during our time together you find yourself in any situation where you are neither learning nor contributing, use your two feet and go somewhere else'.

This approach to learning – free, open, self-run – can be wonderfully enriching, but also unnerving. Participants must accept a new way of learning that involves observing, experiencing, embracing difference, and acknowledging mistakes. In this way, the AoH encounter also represents an emotional journey where anxieties can rise to the surface. In our group, a number of participants – perhaps half a dozen, mainly those working at larger corporations – had come with their own expectations of what they would take away, and by the half-way stage of the week-long encounter, begun to question these precepts: 'where was the manual?', they asked; 'why hadn't the information been systematized?' At one stage, these anxieties threatened to boil over into outright revolt. But on this occasion, our hosts stood firm, recognizing and accepting these concerns, but not veering from their vision that it was up to each participant to contribute and to take from the encounter what they would.

It is here that the art of leadership really comes in to play, as the host perseveres through those periods of chaos by having participatory methodologies such as Open Space built into their DNA. In these moments an effective leader will seek to operate in the background as much as possible, an almost invisible actor whose presence does not influence the way the group chooses to operate; but she must be paying complete attention at all times, observing not just what is said, but what is done and how it is done – sensing the group's energy. It is up to her to know when she must play the role of the chalice bearer, embracing, soothing and calming, and when is the time to intervene as the blade-wielding warrior, nudging, cajoling and, above all, questioning in order that the group might move forward.

Successful leaders are therefore those that are able to harness and catalyze collective knowledge and different talents around a shared purpose, weaving solutions that recognize and value the voices and opinions of the individual and of the collective. Where, previously, we were schooled in Isaac Newton's mantra that it was possible to find singular answers to our problems through objective analysis, now we must accept a more inclusive and dynamic view of the world, which accepts that there is no one single, objective 'solution' or answer and that the observer herself influences the response as a direct result of her expectations or intentions.

The art of leading is an art of hosting. As leaders we learn to sense the flow not only within ourselves and our direct relations but also in our teams of people prototyping the future. We learn to sense when the team may be holding-on too much to the tried-and-tested status quo and need cajoling out of our comfort zones through interventions and provocations that disturb and catalyze.

Like learning to improvise with fellow Jazz musicians, we learn to become masters at sensing how to balance our teams' out-of-the-box envisioning, future searching and chaotic explorations with the need to focus-in and deliver, continuously attuning our chalice-bearing and blade-wielding qualities.

We sense the adaptive cycles of the team and how they resonate with the adaptive cycles of the organization and wider business context. We are forever in a 'leadership laboratory' with unfolding situations continuously honing our leadership capacity to sense, tune-in, listen, open-up and emerge with what is best for the situation at hand, learning as we go.

When we embrace this artful gnosis in our way of working, we find that the only path worth walking is the one that flows with soul. Yet, we also begin to realize how testing this path is for us and our acculturated habits and ego-patterns of behavior. We encounter cynicism from others and also from our own selves. Regularly, our ego-mind will question and throw doubt and fear into the mix while we are dealing with challenges. Our own inner-critic will question why we are not doing things the way we always have done, not sticking to the status quo, taking the easier short-cut rather than seeking a more authentic yet ego-challenging path.

> 'It's not easy, listening to the song in your heart. There are long periods of doubt and uncertainty when you are not even sure if you are doing the right thing.'
> *Anupam Jalote, entrepreneur*

Scilla Elworthy notes that cynicism from ourselves and from others can be a pragmatic ally for us if it compels us to become clearer in our perspectives, our sense of purpose, and our ways of presenting to others what and why we are doing what we are doing. It makes us aware of where others are at and how much we need to reach across to where they are at rather than where we might wish them to be. We need to learn to take this cynicism and criticism as a form of constructive feedback.

As our gnosis deepens, we perceive conflicts and criticisms as gifts for transformation. The tensions they bring help us develop our selves further. Somatic awareness can greatly help here: the more intimate we get with how we feel in our bodymind when experiencing cynicism, criticism or conflict, the more we can allow our bodymind to transform these tensions into insight for ourselves. By noticing the feelings and emotions that well up within us in these challenging situations, we can provide space for the emotions to do their work and release through our subtle energetic body sensations, rather than attempting to suppress or overriding them with our ego-consciousness, stuffing them into our shadow unconscious, only to resurface another time.

In the midst of criticism or conflict, we can bring our attention into the body and sense how we are feeling and where there is tension and where difficult emotions are arising from. It may seem like we do not have the space for such somatic awareness in the heat of the exchange, but this is exactly when we need to be aware. We learn to feel the pain or anxiety in our heart or gut region, and feel how the anger may start to rise up, the hurt may start to expand or the jealousy creeps up in us. As we pause, we do not try and repress this feeling, we learn to become conscious of it, to really feel it. It will not actually transform into anger or rage if we are conscious of it (unless we then consciously decide to be angry) instead, it will actually undertake its own informing intelligence within us. Opening up our awareness beyond the cerebral interpretation of our experience is really powerful for our gnosis.

Yet, this cynicism or conflict can easily undermine us, especially when we are feeling out on a limb, tired and harassed in the thick of it all. Our doubting inner-critic latches on to this cynicism and fuels doubts and anxieties within us that, if allowed to start ruminating out of control, can sap away at our conscious energy, undermining our ego-soul dynamic as the ego starts to dominate amid the fear and doubt. Instead of ensuring our vital energy flows into our deeper awareness, it starts to flow into the ego-chatter, crowding out our other ways of knowing to the extent that we become unbalanced and even more anxious, run-down and soul-sapped. In the heat of it all we can easily react from our old ways of fear, quick-fix response, domination, short-termism, trade-off logic, getting-the-job-done in a less than authentic way. Our inner-critic can then feed on this to further undermine and self-judge as we start to beat ourselves up for not doing the job in the right way, for slipping up and failing as an authentic leader, in our own eyes. Soon we find ourselves in a vicious cycle of cynicism, self-criticism, anxiety, weakening coherence, sense of failure, further dissonance, and so on. Hence, we do need to be aware of cynicism in ourselves and others. We need to catch ourselves through regular practices of self-awareness and renewal amid our busy schedule.

The world is full of cynics at every turn; people saying it how they see it from their jaundice perspective or from a place of jealously, competitiveness, political backstabbing, etc. This is the very real situation we are attempting to lead in – like it or not. And so we need regular pauses, conscious breathing, moments of reflection, meditative periods, and such like, to review how we are doing as well as regular breaks out of the office to renew ourselves. This is an important part of leading – taking personal responsibility for checking-in with ourselves.

Conscious breathing is a great aid here, as is creating space at the end of each day to review what has gone on for us, what we need to process and what we can let go of, while reaffirming our enthusiasm and courage. Likewise, a day out of the office in nature can be very rejuvenating for the soul and for our overall bodymind coherence. We often feel we need to be at the coalface all the time, even allowing emails and work calls to creep into the weekend, but this undermines our own adaptive cycle of creativity, development and renewal, and undermines our viability to lead authentically, in turn undermining our organization's gnosis.

At an organizational level, we may learn the art of creating a space for tensions to arise and be held without the need for premature fixing. We can suggest a meeting without a fixed agenda or goal in mind so we can openly share how the tensions feel, or explore cynicism through open dialogue or deep listening, or we can suggest a walk in the park or a lunch outside the office somewhere to discuss the challenges in a non-confrontation way. Or we may wish to sleep on it all and give it some space and allow the cynicism or tension to be seen from different perspectives, empathized with and explored for the insightful gem it may bring us.

TIP

SOUL SPACE AT THE END OF THE DAY

Rich meals accompanied with alcohol and coffee after a hard day's work are seen as quite normal in business life these days, especially when sharing a meal with business colleagues, clients or networking after an evening event or staying at a hotel while away on business. But this is the last thing our bodymind needs before bed time. We need to allow enough time for the meal to digest well before we start to wind down ahead of retiring to bed. Ideally, we make time in our schedule for some light exercise before going to bed. We get changed out of our work clothes into something more comfortable and go for a ten minute walk in the fresh air or perhaps a light jog and a stretch. After this, we might take a shower as a way of letting go of the busy day before getting ready for bed. Then, we can do some gentle exercises for a couple of minutes (longer if possible). For instance, some gentle yoga postures or some Qi gong or T'ai Chi movements. These gentle movements help us bring our awareness into the body while our thinking mind starts to quieten down.

Upon getting into bed, we remain sitting upright in a comfortable posture with our back straight and our legs crossed (or whatever feels most comfortable). We then engage in a few rounds of conscious breathing. This calms us down and allows our sympathetic and parasympathetic body systems to cohere. Then we dedicate some quiet moments of reflection to run through the day from start to finish, briefly going over the interactions we had, the emotions and experiences, noticing when we get caught up in a particular event or exchange that occurred and the tensions and felt-senses it provokes within us. It can be useful to have a journal or notebook by the side of the bed so we can jot down the key points of the day in terms of what went well, what we learnt, what we could do better in the future, what was particularly uncomfortable or challenging. Or we can just sit with this reflective exercise without needing to write anything down.

Once we have adequately reviewed the day, we can then do a few rounds of conscious breathing to allow our thoughts of the day to lessen their grip on our awareness. Then, when we feel more still, we can place our hands gently over our heart area while doing conscious breathing, and then do a few rounds of 'heart breathing' as if we are breathing through our heart area.

It is a great practice to then think of things we really love, as well as the everyday things we are grateful for in our lives. These can be universal things such as the air we breathe, the sunlight that gives us warmth and makes the plants we eat grow, the natural beauty of the world, the food and shelter we have, our loved ones, and the little things that make us smile. If we start to struggle with what to focus on in terms of grateful things or we notice our mind getting caught up in thoughts of the day, we just bring our attention back into our breathing through the heart and feel the warmth of our heart and a feeling of love flowing through our entire body. At that point we can then either lie down in bed and start to focus on the energy sensations and feelings in our body (as per the Yoga Nidra tip explored early) or remain upright and engage in sitting meditation for a few minutes by noticing our thoughts appearing in our thinking mind while developing deeper awareness of the stillness beyond the thoughts. Soon we will feel ready for some quality sleep which will rejuvenate us far more than if we had gone to bed with a full stomach of rich food, wine, beer and/or coffee.

>◆◆◆

When we start to become more masterful in our ego-soul dynamic as leaders and change agents, the boundaries between our work-life and leisure-life may begin to become more porous, because our work becomes our passion, and the soul-flow we experience when being in service of our passion no longer feels like 'work'. Hence, we need to be ever-conscious of ensuring the right balance in our lives of working, playing, regularly exercising, eating healthily, fostering deep nurturing relations and regular practices to rejuvenate and deeply renew ourselves.

By way of summarizing this module on leadership, here are some characteristic qualities of fear-based leading (old logic) compared with the new logic of courage-based leading from the heart:

FEAR-BASED LEADING		COURAGE-BASED LEADING
Authoritarian	⇨	Emancipation
Leader-follower relation	⇨	Co-creative relation
Motivated by power	⇨	Motivated by passion and purpose
Blame culture	⇨	Compassionate culture
Risk-averse	⇨	Pioneering
Adversarial	⇨	Inspirational
Competitive	⇨	Empathic
Command-and-control	⇨	Improvisational
Dominator-mode	⇨	Partnership-mode

TIP

EQUINE FACILITATED LEARNING

The ancient art of horsemanship has been traced back to 8000 BC. Over the centuries horses have become domesticated in part due to their amicable nature. Less than one hundred years ago horses were our transport, our agricultural support and our assistants in warfare. As machines took over their jobs as workhorses and warhorses, equines have become our recreation, our partners and our pets. But now, amid this time of Great Transition, a growing number of equine specialists have been exploring how horses have a role to play in teaching us about courageous leadership in practice.

When we engage with a horse, the horse's biological make-up requires us to become an authentic leader in order for the horse to feel safe. As soon as we start to connect with a horse she or he will be sizing us up, asking: who is leading? When building a relationship with a horse there can be a fine line between being over assertive, and not assertive enough. The honest feedback the horse will give can help us find the middle path. Trust, courage, congruency and humility are all leadership qualities we can learn from working with horses.

Working with horses in this way has become known as 'Equine Facilitated Learning'. One such equine specialist I have had the pleasure of engaging with is Sue Blagburn. (Note 15) With the help of her extraordinary horses, Sue Blagburn applies whole-systems learning, systemic coaching and phenomenology to help us cultivate our awareness in how we are being. (Note 16) This provides leaders the opportunity to learn about themselves and others through experiential and embodied learning with horses. As she notes, 'We enter a field of no wrong or right doing, a completely non-judgmental space for self-development, an environment of safety, trust, confidentiality and openness; and then the horses do most of the work.'

Blagburn encourages participants to step out of their normal comfort zone - many may not have handled a horse before - learning through being coached how to lead a horse without any force or dominance. The horse is always given the choice of connecting, engaging and working with the participant or not as the case may be.

When learning to partner and lead horses without words and without force we begin to develop all of our natural ways of being, while gaining a direct and embodied experience of what it feels like when we lessen the dominance of our ego-awareness. The horses provide accurate and instant feedback through responses based on how safe and energized they feel in the participant's presence; the horses simply respond to how the participant really is, in the present moment. The horses pick up and listen not to the participant's agenda, status, or outer persona but to their overall bodymind resonance, body language and inner intent. And so the horses act as mirrors to the feelings and emotions we experience in our everyday work-life.

The word guide means 'someone who can find paths through unexplored and unknown territory' and in this regard the horses are insightful guides for our personal and organizational journeys, teaching us to pay attention and stay connected with the present moment, and how to stay focused on a goal or an obstacle without overly analyzing or judging. This provides a foundational space and grounded experience to cultivate courageous leadership beyond the ego-imposed limitations of positional authority and control.

REFLECTIVE QUESTIONS

Over the past few days at work, can you recall when you were leading either in a more fear-based way and or in a more courage-based way?

Can you recall how a particularly challenging situation unfolded, and how it felt for you?

How often do you create space in your schedule specifically to renew yourself, to have space and time to relax, contemplate, reflect and recharge?

Ask yourself if you are able to have the self-disciple to dedicate at least five minutes 'soul space' at the end of every day to reflect and also to cultivate an attitude of gratitude. Do you feel your personal development and organizational success warrants this five minutes at the end of each day?

How would you describe yourself as a leader - what qualities, strengths and characteristics do you embody?

When was the last time you undertook a 360 degree feedback with members of your team and direct reports? Could you arrange to do an informal one next week?

Are there other leaders in different parts of your organization and in other organizations you work with who you could get to know and take time out with to share in a heart-felt authentic way, say over lunch or an evening drink, on a regular basis, to gain a different perspective on dealing with challenges in your work-life?

Think of three leaders in the world that really inspire you, or that you greatly admire. What is it that you admire in them?

Be still for a few moments, relax and breathe deep. Meditate on this question for a few moments, 'How may I serve?'

MODULE **SEVEN**

ALCHEMY

'PERHAPS THE GREATEST CHANGE THAT
WE HUMANS ARE EXPERIENCING IS OUR
RISING CONSCIOUSNESS. TO BE
CONSCIOUS MEANS TO BE FULLY AWAKE
AND MINDFUL, TO SEE REALITY MORE
CLEARLY, AND TO MORE FULLY
UNDERSTAND ALL THE CONSEQUENCES
– SHORT TERM AND LONG TERM – OF
OUR ACTIONS.'
JOHN MACKEY, CEO WHOLE FOODS AND RAJ SISODIA,
CO-FOUNDER OF CONSCIOUS CAPITALISM

SEVERAL CENTURIES BEFORE THE BIRTH of Christ, ancient Western and Eastern civilizations contained sophisticated wisdom traditions sharing similar themes and threads across geographies and cultures. An enduring and influential tradition is that of alchemy. Alchemy is thought to have originated in Egypt (The Chem being an old name for Egypt) yet its roots can be found in ancient shamanic and tantric practices inherent in indigenous cultures the world over. While there are many levels of esoteric richness to alchemy, what is relevant to us here are the insights it provides our journey of self-realization through the mastery of our ego-soul dynamic.

Through the concocting communion of the opposing tensions of our ego and soul, our bodymind becomes an alchemic vessel for our personal gnosis. The alchemic wedding or communion of our inner masculine principles (also referred to as 'yang' qualities in ancient Chinese Taoism or the 'animus' by Carl Jung) and inner feminine principles (also referred to as 'yin' qualities or 'anima') within our psyche provides for a transformation in our consciousness from a state dominated by ego projections, fears and lurking shadow unconscious complexes, to a more fully integrated ego-soul awareness.

Through the alchemic heat of our enduring quest for self-realization, our ego raises its vibration so as to allow for harmonization with our soul. As a result, our daily conscious awareness opens out into the richer depth and breadth of our true nature rooted in the ground of our being, the World Soul of Nature (anima mundi). The soul always has been and always will be immersed within this deeper World Soul; we are simply opening up to this awareness in a conscious and comprehensible way with the help of our ego-soul dynamic. As Jungian analyst and author Anne Baring notes, 'the soul is not in us: we are in the Soul.' [Note 1] It is in this conscious state of awareness that we embody a deep sense of participating in the web of life where we sense every aspect as inter-related with every other aspect, just as the ancient Vedic cosmology of The Net of Indra portrays a web of golden threads weaving together jewels each reflecting and containing the whole web. It is here that we innately know that regenerative business is the only viable future for us.

Our bodymind, soul and spirit resonate with the spirit of life flowing with Sophia, the wisdom of the world. Our actions and interactions follow this flow by surrendering and being in service to the flow as we learn to become ever more conscious of our participatory, co-creative contribution in this life; a humbling yet awe-inspiring venture. It is what Joseph Campbell points to when he notes, 'The individual has to find what electrifies, what enlivens the heart, this is the salvation of your life. That means putting yourself in accord with Nature…When you are in accord with Nature, Nature will yield up its bounty and every sacred place is the place where eternity shines through time.' (Note 2)

What we have explored in this book is how our personal gnosis reinforces and is reinforced by our organizational gnosis, where ways of being and doing inform and inspire each other during our unfolding, enriching journey toward regenerative business.

By way of summarizing what we have covered in the previous modules, let us list some core yin-yang principles present at both personal and organizational levels, so that we can allow for an alchemic integration of these yin-yang qualities within us and our organizations; learning to sense when more of one dynamic is needed or a little more of the other:

YIN QUALITIES		YANG QUALITIES
Inter-relationality	∞	Reductive categorization
Receptivity	∞	Responsiveness
Inner-sense	∞	Outer-action
Intuitive wisdom	∞	Rational reasoning
Cyclic, spiraling, eco-systemic inclusiveness	∞	Linear, focused, siloed specialization
Cooperation and synergy	∞	Competition and trade-off
Listening, feeling, contemplating, being	∞	Action-orientated, purposeful doing
Open-mode, creative, playful	∞	Closed-mode, goal-driven
Back-loop of radical innovation and rebirth	∞	Front-loop of incremental efficiencies
Communicate, empathize and transform	∞	Question, examine, analyze and solve
Heart and soul	∞	Head and ego

A living, regenerative business needs to hold these yin-yang tensions and allow a deeper wisdom to emerge from what these tensions yield amid our ever-changing business context. Yet, let us be reminded of the timeless wisdom of Lao Tzu, 'Know the male yet keep to the female' [(Note 3)], likewise the genius Einstein knew that the yang of the rational mind is useful to us only as faithful servant to the intuitive soul. The more we open up to the soul, the more Sophia flows through us, and the more we fully embrace the regenerative river of Life.

As well as the ancient yin-yang image from the East (symbolizing the communion of feminine and masculine aspects within Life) there is also the ancient alchemic image of the hexagon, found predominantly in the West and Middle East. This hexagon is the interweaving of two triangles representing the communion of feminine (the triangle pointing downward, also representing the element water) and masculine (the triangle pointing upward, also representing the element fire). [(Note 4)] This is the wisdom of Nature within and all around us; it's just a case of our attuning to it, activating this timeless wisdom for today.

Wisdom is a way of perceiving and attending to life – a way of living that involves 'being and doing' in a natural, soulful, loving and graceful way. When we allow our true nature to radiate through us, we become transparent to the transcendent, and intimate with the immanent, soulfulness of this inter-relating ever-changing rich and wise world; our being infuses our doing as we become who we were born to be.

This true nature within us has an underlying essence, yet also a dynamic emergence to it. The more we whole-heartedly open up to the diversity of experience - with all the subpersonalities, repressed desires, memories, contradictory impulses, instinctual urges and archetypal influences that arise in us – the more we allow this essence to flow emergently through our work. This goes hand-in-hand with our organizational sense of purpose, strategic and operational approaches, methods of communication and day-to-day conventions all becoming emergent, creative, authentic and purposeful.

As we come to know ourselves more intimately, the way we relate to others is enriched. How we communicate with each other becomes less hurried, impatient, defensive and anxious, and more authentic and consciously aware. This helps us sense the true nature in others, to be patient, attentive and empathic in our relations, and for others to drop their guard a little and feel safer in opening up in their sharing with us. As we learn to sense the true nature in ourselves and in others we realize there is an essential ground of being that permeates everything all the time. We all have the same essential ground of being within us, each of us manifesting our own unique expression of it through our soulful radiance. By truly listening to the other person, by transcending our masks, projections, judgements and 'what's-in-it-for-me' thinking, we allow an opening up to this ground of all being.

'The true ground of all being is the infinite, intangible, spirit that infuses all living beings'
David Bohm, physicist

Let us pause for a moment.

Recall a recent conversation at work, and reflect on how we were listening and sharing. If we are brutally honest here, we may well be able to recall when we were not actually being our authentic selves, perhaps skewing the conversation through our judgements, personal agendas, defensive positioning, desires to get our point across, manipulating our presentation in a way that 'sells' our view in the best light. In some respects this is normal human sociality, yet if 'over done' it hinders the emergence of deeper soul-to-soul improvisational sharing.

To be vulnerable, undefended, open-hearted and free from ego-encroachments requires our conscious attention, determination and courage. And when we do open up whole-heartedly and put our agendas and judgements to one side, the other person (consciously or unconsciously) will sense this and feel more able to open up themselves, inviting in an opening for soulful sharing. The life-blood of our firms of the future is this soulful sharing through the day-to-day conversations, the adhoc feedback, the listening intently, the corridor chat, the collaborative gatherings, the stillness within meetings, and empathic email responses.

'To be here requires attention, listening, and gazing deeply without assaulting each thing seen with a conclusion. The silence here is not just in the 'what has been', it is most deliciously waiting, too, in the 'what will be'.
Cheryl Sanders-Sardello, phenomenologist

The continual challenge is to remain grounded and centered as situations unfold. A loving interest in each unfolding moment provides for an active creativity which is calm yet energised, patient yet passionate, devoted yet tolerant. (Note 5)

Amid these times of upheaval and challenge, we are midwifing the birthing of our authentic selves, simultaneously midwifing a metamorphosis of our humanity within our organizations, global community and more-than-human world. And birthing always comes with surrender, pain and then the beginning of a deeper, wider vista of remembering why we are here: to live in love and wisdom.

'Awakening to the original seed of one's soul and hearing it speak may not be easy. How do we recognize its voice; what signals does it give? Before we can address these questions, we need to notice our own deafness, the obstructions that make us hard of hearing; the reductionism, the literalism, the scientism of our so-called common sense… For the soul is not a measureable entity, not a substance, not a force – even if we are called by the force [of its] curious thought, devotional feeling, suggestive intuition, and daring imagination.'
James Hillman, psychologist [Note 6]

'We misunderstand love because we have become obsessed with control; we silence the reasons of the heart because we have chosen to follow a path of heartless knowledge, no matter where it takes us; we do not adore because we insist that every thing and every person be of use to us; we do not wonder because we reduce the real to the measureable; we do not care because we have come to believe that it profits a man or woman well above the prime rate to trade the soul for a piece of the action.'
Sam Keen, philosopher [Note 7]

The cultural context within which we find ourselves is severely lop-sided. Our dominant socio-economic paradigm twists us down pathways that undermine our soulful engagement while fanning the flames of our engulfing ego-centricity. In turn we erode our relations, our communities and the wider fabric of life. Our acculturated perspectives have, by and large, become skewed down economic cul-de-sacs that draw us away from who we naturally and authentically are. Consumerism feeds off and perpetuates our egotism with fickle desires never truly satisfied, fragmenting us from sources of real and lasting happiness. We perceive each other and the wider ensemble of Nature through a short-termist, materialistic lens, that desacralizes life for short-lived highs. We busy ourselves patching up symptoms while neglecting the root causes. We recklessly burn our future for today's party, and call it 'progress'.

Collectively, we have become unwise. But there are signs of a Great Transition afoot and each of us, through our relationships, and our sense of purpose, passion and compassion, can catalyze these shifts in our organizations across the globe. It's time to stand up for what we know in our hearts to be right.

We are at a critical time, a supreme moment, a cross roads, where we either open up to our potential as Homo sapiens (wise beings), or we continue to sow and reap the seeds of our demise, undermining the greatness of Life. Our attention is a moral act; our choices have moral implications. Every moment opens up the opportunity to attend to life with love or fear, with grace or dis-ease. How we attend to the world shapes our world in-turn shaping us.

> 'To see a World in a Grain of Sand
> And a Heaven in a Wild Flower,
> Hold Infinity in the palm of your hand
> And Eternity in an hour.'
> *William Blake, poet*

APPENDIX ONE

FUTURE-FIT ORGANIZATIONAL HEALTH-CHECK QUESTIONS

(NOTE 1)

(PLEASE NOTE THAT THERE IS SOME OVERLAP AND REPETITION IN THESE HEALTH-CHECK SECTION AREAS OFFERED HERE, AND THIS IS BY NO WAY A DEFINITIVE OR COMPLETE SET OF QUESTIONS. FEEL FREE TO APPLY AND ADAPT THESE QUESTIONS FOR YOUR OWN ORGANIZATION AS YOU SEE FIT.)

PURPOSE & CHARACTER

What is the purpose of the organization?

How does this purpose sit within the current context of our world?

What are the wider contextual challenges and opportunities this purpose calls upon and encounters?

How is this purpose understood in terms of organizational vitality and future-fit?

What about in terms of competition, survival and short-term viability?

What are the internal threats/opportunities within the organization in terms of its current ability to deliver this purpose?

How is this purpose understood in terms of broader stakeholder, social, environmental, economic factors?

How far along the road is the organization in aligning its intention of purpose with its culture, values, ways of operating and behaving?

Is there a tension between holding the intention of purpose and being profitable? How is this tension held in the business?

Have there been any key historic events or periods of transformation that have affected the organization's sense of purpose in the last few years?

How does the Exec team understand and commit to fulfilling the purpose of the organization? How is this reflected in their remit, accountability and approach?

How does this sense of purpose relate to the wider organizational culture and behavioral dynamics (within the organization and across the stakeholder ecosystem)?

What differentiates the organization from its peers?

Are there homogenous and heterogeneous qualities across the organization?

What type of characteristics and qualities fit with the organization and which do not? What type of person fits-in and what type does not?

Are there any regular activities to engage teams across the organization (and stakeholders beyond) in sensing the deeper purpose and understanding how it relates to respective areas of influence/accountability?

How is this sense of purpose conveyed in internal and external communications?

How is the purpose related to governance philosophy, principles and practices across the organization?

How does company strategy align with the purpose? How is the strategy disseminated across different areas of the business?

What about company performance reporting, is financial performance integrated with social and environmental factors? How does this reporting approach roll-up and then disseminate?

Is there a governance approach for helping personal purpose, roles and focus to align with organizational purpose? Is this hierarchic or self-organizing?

How do performance reviews and remunerations relate with this purpose?

VALUES, BEHAVIORS, COMMUNICATION, DECISION MAKING, TENSION TRANFORMATION

Does the company have a clear set of values that are translated into ground rules of (un)acceptable behaviors?

Is there a conflict resolution process and how does this relate with everyday tension transformation?

Are there explicit and clear practices to allow for these values to be lived out?

How would you describe decision making – bureaucratic, hierarchic and top-down or open, distributed and inclusive?

Is there a tension between top down decisions and distributive collective decision making? How is this tension held in the business?

Would you say the culture is one of embracing experimentation and continuous learning or one of prescriptive cook-book approaches and tried-and-tested regulations? Or perhaps it is a blend of both?

How are formal meetings, informal conversations and organization-wide communications conducted throughout the organization?

How would you describe the style of communications on a continuum between formal and informal?

Are tensions perceived as healthy in terms of transcending toward emergent outcomes, greater resiliency and making space for further tensions to emerge as a quality of co-creativity?

Is there a schism between external public relations messaging of organizational culture and the shop-floor workings, office politics and gossip?

How do values and culture differentiate across geographies? How does any differentiation and localization inter-relate with global organizational culture?

What is morale like in the organization? How do retention levels compare with similar organizations? Are there pockets of higher turn-over or lower morale, and of higher morale? How is this related to leadership, employee engagement, team morale and people development?

How is training and development undertaken?

Is there recognition of the relationship between personal awareness and collective effectiveness?

Are personal awareness activities (contemplative or somatic practices such as mindfulness or yoga) embraced as conducive to the organization's performance?

Is there recognition of the contribution of self-awareness/ self-development around the dynamics of 'power over' shifting to 'power with'?

What education/awareness is provided around personal gnosis (social, somatic and soulful awareness) and its relation with purposefulness, effectiveness and resilience?

COLLABORATION & INNOVATION

Is the organization siloed, matrixed, networked or inter-relational?

Are there mind-sets that resist sharing between departments, functions and teams?

What about KPIs, do the KPIs encourage cross-collaboration?

Have people developed an appreciation and skill for working in a collaborative and creative way? Can you provide examples?

Is creativity and innovation seen as the province of a select group of people/functions or is it disseminated throughout? Is this bottom-up and locally-attuned or top-down controlled, or a blend of both?

How does the ability to adapt and create at the individual and team level play out in practice?

Are 'intuition', 'sensing and responding' and 'collective intelligence' recognized as guides for emerging ideas, inspiration and the formulation of plans?

How often do teams of diverse stakeholders get together for the purpose of enriching collaboration and innovation without pre-defined targets/outcomes?

Is the organizational boundary permeable or tightly controlled, or a blend of both?

Are suppliers/partners chosen in terms of how they relate with the organizational purpose?

How are suppliers/partners engaged with: tight prescriptive management or flexible, adaptive relations built on trust and sharing?

Are open innovation and creative commons approaches welcomed or feared? Are there any examples?

How does the tension of competition and collaboration play out within the cultural dynamics?

How are 'competitors' perceived and engaged with?

What about wider stakeholders such as local communities, pressure groups, think tanks, social media forums, thought leader networks, industry bodies, etc.?

RELATIONSHIPS & INTERPERONAL DYNAMICS

Do people openly engage in authentic and meaningful conversations about their passions and values?

Are people encouraged to - and feel safe to – provide informal feedback?

Are there opportunities for developing skills in ways to powerfully deal with conflict?

What % of people are trained in dialogue and conflict transformation?

Are there peer reviews and 360 degree feedback processes in place?

Beyond performance reviews, how do peer-based reviews at a collective/team level embed in to day-to-day operations?

Are there team away days? How often, and how are they facilitated?

Is there an organizational intrinsic 'feeling' about 'doing the right thing'?

What is the office gossip? Is 'positive gossip' encouraged through the sharing of positive stories and the rewarding/ recognition of sharing, assisting and being appreciative of others contributions?

Is there autonomy at the individual role level for people to 'sense and respond' in their own ways while openly engaging with others to effect change?

Is there a level of freedom for personal training and development as well as organizational/functional specific training?

What daily practices are in place to cultivate a creative, collaborative, sharing environment?

Is there a process for potential recruits, new joiners and existing staff to check-in and sense a resonance with the organizational sense of purpose?

Are there activities for people at the personal and collective level to help awareness of egotistic behaviors and how to transcend them? What about soulful behaviors, how are these recognized and encouraged?

Is there caring support for people who no longer feel aligned to the organization's sense of purpose?

ENVIRONMENT

Are work spaces comfortable, warm, inviting, open spaces or mechanized and utilitarian?

Does the working environment awaken creativity, collaboration and flourishing, or deaden it?

Is there an awareness of infrastructure, spatial design and layout in relation to personal and organizational effectiveness?

Is there an awareness of Sick Building Syndrome, Intelligent

Building and Biophilic Workplace within Estates Management, Human Resources and day-to-day office management?

Are there office managers? What is their role and contribution on a day-to-day basis?

Are there quiet places intentionally allocated in the building where people can go to reflect, let-go and revitalize?

What about creative spaces, white board areas, casual meeting spots?

Is time and space scheduled for creative thinking, brainstorming, and contemplative activities as well as somatic and fitness activities?

Is food provided at work? If so, what criteria are in place?

Are people encouraged to clearly delineate between their home/leisure life and work life or encouraged to be open about activities, pursuits and interested beyond work?

Is home and remote working established within the culture? How is this managed?

Are in-between times kept sacred for quiet, reflective time or are busy diaries viewed as the norm?

Are walks in nature, time outside, retreats and other sessions out of the office encouraged?

Is a diverse network of peers and activities outside the organization viewed as healthy or as a distraction?

MANGEMENT MINDSET - MECHANISTIC TO LIVING

What proportion of the senior management team would you say view the organization as a living, evolving entity, and what proportion prefer a mechanistic perspective?

Is 'systems-thinking' recognized across senior management levels?

Is there a 'systems' understanding of the organization's ecosystem of stakeholders?

How would you describe the boundaries and relations of the organization with other parties – are they boundaries of competition, bargaining and trade-off to be tightly managed and controlled, or are they perceived as dynamic inter-relations offering synergy through mind-share and joint understanding at local and global levels?

Is planning and budgeting fixed, tightly managed and prescriptive? How does it work in practice?

Are scenario planning and iterative planning approaches regularly embraced?

What planning tolerance is there for emergence, prototyping and adaptations?

What does growth mean and look like for the organization? What about transformation, innovation, reconfiguration and renewal?

Are different parts of the organization at different stages of growth/reconfiguration?

Is there a felt sense of the dynamic, emergent, ever-changing environment of the organization or a desire to 'control and predict', to stick hard-and-fast to detailed plans and budgets for clarity and control?

How is power distributed across the work environment?

What about approaches to facilitation, co-participation, learning through experimentation and embracing failure?

How are targets cascaded? What is the % of quantified versus qualified targets, and short term versus medium term targets?

How do linear, homogenized aspects of the operations inter-relate with more emergent and self-organizing aspects?

APPENDIX TWO

THE FUTURE-FIT
BUSINESS BENCHMARK

WHY DO WE NEED TO MEASURE
PROGRESS TOWARD FUTURE-FITNESS?

THE EMINENT SCIENTIST LORD KELVIN famously said *if you cannot measure it, you cannot improve it.* To encourage and empower companies to become future-fit, we need to equip those who lead and invest in them with the means to measure their progress – and to identify where they are falling short.

DON'T ENVIRONMENTAL AND SOCIAL PERFORMANCE METRICS ALREADY EXIST?

Today, companies typically measure environmental and social performance in one of three ways: relative to a previous year, relative to today's best practice, or relative to short-term goals the company has set itself (see figure). All three approaches reward gradual improvements to the status quo, rather than meaningful progress toward a desired future state. So even a poorly performing company with a completely unsustainable business model can look like it's doing well if it happens to be doing better than last year, or better than its peers.

To see whether a company is helping – rather than hindering – society's transition to a flourishing future, we must assess the gap between where it is now and where it needs to be. Measuring progress relative to peers, to the past, or to short-term goals is not enough to assess future-fitness.

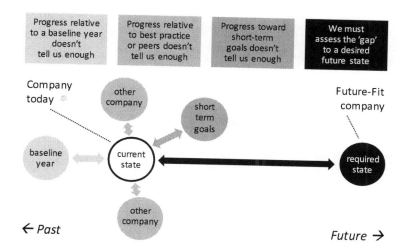

WHY IS THE FUTURE-FIT BUSINESS BENCHMARK DIFFERENT?

The Future-Fit Business Benchmark takes a new approach. Not one focused on where business is today, but on where it needs to be. It is grounded in a scientific definition of how the world works: one that identifies the minimum threshold of performance any company must reach, across all critical social and environmental issues, if it is to help – rather than hinder – society's transition to a flourishing future.

HOW DOES IT WORK?

The Future-Fit Business Benchmark answers two questions. First: *how would we know a future-fit business if we saw one?* To answer this, the Benchmark offers a set of clear goals that any company must reach, no matter what its size or sector, to gain its 'entry ticket' to a flourishing future. This gives companies a clear destination to aim for, but it doesn't tell them how far they still have to go.

That brings us to the second question: *how can we tell how far away a business is today from becoming truly future-fit?* For business leaders to prioritize effectively, and for investors to make meaningful performance comparisons across companies, we need a way to measure progress toward the destination. So the Benchmark also offers a set of Key Fitness Indicators, or KFIs – one for every Future-Fit Goal. Each KFI, expressed as a simple percentage, enables a company to measure the gap between where it is now and where it needs to be.

HOW IS THE BENCHMARK BEING USED?

The Benchmark is published under a Creative Commons License, free for any company to use. A first draft set of Future-Fit Goals was published in October 2014, and since then over a hundred academic and industry experts have contributed to its improvement. A range of companies – from small social enterprises to global corporations – have started using the Future-Fit Goals and the thinking behind them to realign their strategic priorities. The first full Benchmark release – containing a refined set of goals, together with a complementary set of KFIs – is now available as you read this.

WHERE CAN I FIND OUT MORE ABOUT THIS BENCHMARK?

You can download the latest version of the Future-Fit Business Benchmark from futurefitbusiness.org, where you can also find case studies and other supporting materials to help persuade others of the need – and opportunity – to become future-fit. The Future-Fit Foundation, the non-profit organization behind the Benchmark, is committed to improving it over time, so all constructive feedback is welcome and encouraged.

NOTES

MODULE ONE: A METAMORPHOSIS IN OUR MIDST

NOTE 1: These half a dozen paragraphs are edited from a paper co-authored by Anton Chernikov and Giles Hutchins entitled *Redefining The Nature of Business for the Millennial Age*, for more on this see http://www.exponentials.co.uk/#!opinion-paper/ctmx

NOTE 2: I make no apologies for using this quote in my last two books (the only quote I use in all three books – I think). It is a favourite quote of mine because it's a no holes-barred statement from a first-rate business man who successfully ran an international manufacturing organization, leaving as his legacy an inspiring corporate case study - Interface the world's largest carpets manufacturer. For more on Ray Andersen see *Confessions of a Radical Industrialist*

NOTE 3: Paul Hawken's comment as part of his 2009 Commencement Address to the University of Portland see http://www.up.edu/commencement/default.aspx?cid=9456

MODULE TWO: FIRMS OF THE FUTURE

NOTE 1: See John Seddon's *Freedom from Command & Control*, the quote can be found on p23

NOTE 2: For more on the term 'redesigning for resilience' and its application to business transformation, see *The Nature of Business*

NOTE 3: For more on this see Nassim Taleb's *Antifragile*

NOTE 4: For more on the historic influences, symptoms and causes of our current carcinogenic logic see *The Illusion of Separation*

NOTE 5: cited p23 *The Illusion of Separation*

NOTE 6: See Alain de Botton's *Status Anxiety* which is entertaining, yet disturbing and illuminating

NOTE 7: This paragraph is edited from p102 *The Nature of Business*

NOTE 8: For this quote and others on regenerative business, plus more general information see http://www.regenterprise.org/regeneration/

NOTE 9: For more on Biomimicry for Creative Innovation see www.businessinspiredbynature.com

NOTE 10: Firm of the future 'ways of doing' are covered in *The Nature of Business*

NOTE 11: For more on this study by the Global LAMP Index see http://www.lampindex.com/

NOTE 12: More detail on the Adnams case study can be found in *The Nature of Business*

NOTE 13: For more on this see p56 *Reinventing Organizations*

NOTE 14: For more on open innovation see http://www.openinnovation.eu/open-innovation/

NOTE 15: For more on the Whole Foods case study see *Conscious Capitalism*

NOTE 16: For more on the Virgin Group case study see *The Nature of Business*

NOTE 17: For more on the shift toward a regenerative society see p283 *The Necessary Revolution*

NOTE 18: For more on the Ecover case study see *The Nature of Business*

NOTE 19: This example came from *The Nature of Business*

NOTE 20: For more on Future Search workshops see the work of Martin Weisbord and Sandra Janoff of the Future Search Network, and this paper here http://www.marvinweisbord.com/wp-content/uploads/2010/04/Future%20Search%20Perspectives.pdf

NOTE 21: For more on Container Store see *Conscious Capitalism*

NOTE 22: For a more detailed case study of Tata Group see *The Nature of Business*

NOTE 23: This section is taken from *The Nature of Business*

NOTE 24: Panarchy is a rich and important aspect of regenerative logic, for more on this see the book *Panarchy* by Lance H. Gunderson and C.S. Holling

NOTE 25: For more on this see p60 of *The Nature of Business*

NOTE 26: This youtube link provides more information on the dynamics of the adaptive cycle https://www.youtube.com/watch?v=NN5a6DoNUYg

NOTE 27: For more on this see p60 of *The Nature of Business*

NOTE 28: For more on this read *What We Learned in the Rainforest*

NOTE 29: Poiesis is a term used by ancient Greek philosophers (Plato and Aristotle, for instance) and more recently by the German philosopher Martin Heidegger, as a way of describing the creative, self-presenting, process of our becoming in and through the world. It is through this poiesis that our soul animates, informs and enriches our lives. For more on poiesis as the language of the soul see *Poiesis* by Stephen Levine, also see http://www.jkp.com/uk/poiesis.html

NOTE 30: For more on bio-rhythms see https://en.wikipedia.org/wiki/Biorhythm

NOTE 31: For more on Mac Macartney's work and his journey toward authentic leadership see *Finding Earth Finding Soul*

NOTE 32: There is one such benchmark that is seeking to do this, it is called The Future-Fit Business Benchmark and it sets out 20 future-fit goals that together define the line in the sand any company must reach, to ensure it in no way hinders society's progress toward a sustainable future. See more on this in Appendix 2 of this book, and also visit http://futurefitbusiness.org/

MODULE THREE: SHIFTING THE LOGIC

NOTE 1: For a more detailed coverage of this see Abraham Maslow's books *Toward a Psychology of Being* and *Motivation and Personality*

NOTE 2: For more on William Torbert's action logic levels of consciousness see https://www.saybrook.edu/rethinkingcomplexity/posts/11-23-11/what-kind-leader-are-you ; for more on Jean Gebster's Integralism see http://integralism.com/

integralism-definition_what-is-integral-jean-gebser-and-five-structures-of-consciousness_85.html ; for more on Ken Wilber's Integral Theory see http://joinintegrallife.com/what-is-integral/ ; for more on Jenny Wade's application of Integral Theory see https://www.integrallife.com/contributors/jenny-wade ; for Clare Graves, Don Beck and Christopher Cowan's Spiral Dynamics theory see http://spiraldynamics.org/ ; for Frederic Laloux's Evolutionary-Teal work in *Reinventing Organizations* see http://www.reinventingorganizations.com/ ; and for more on Richard Barrett's seven levels of consciousness for leaders see https://www.valuescentre.com/mapping-values/barrett-model

NOTE 3: 'Inter-being' is a deep understanding that life is inter-relational and participatory: physically, energetically, and psychically. And with this deeply felt understanding of the interconnectedness of life, we realize that what we do to one aspect of life whether inside ourselves or through our relations with others and the wider world, cause ripples through the whole inter-relational matrix of life. This helps us develop what has been referred to as Collaborative Intelligence where we sense the inter-relational participatory nature of our ever-changing context. At an organizational level, this manifests as the recognition that each organization is inter-dependent with a myriad of inter-related stakeholders including our wider economic, social and environmental ecology. Undermining or alienating one group of stakeholders or aspect of our environment in order to maximize short-term returns for ourselves or our shareholders may provide superficial quick-wins but it inevitably pollutes our inter-relationality and undermines our regenerative potential. As our ego-soul dynamic and gnosis at personal and organizational levels enhances, we strive to serve all of life beyond the logic of trade-offs, and in-so-doing opening up our perceptual horizon to richer vistas of value creation potential, synergistic relations and purposeful business that create the conditions conducive for life to flourish.

NOTE 4: For more about the rising dominance of ego-awareness and the role this has played in our socio-economic logic and Western history see *The Illusion of Separation*

NOTE 5: For more on this see p46 of Abraham Maslow's *Towards a Psychology of Being* or see Richard Barrett's *Evolutionary Coaching*

NOTE 6: For more on Richard Barrett's extensive work in this space see the books *The Values-Driven Organization* and *The New Leadership Paradigm*, also see https://www.valuescentre.com/

NOTE 7: For more on Otto Scharmer's Theory U see https://www.presencing.com/theoryu

NOTE 8: For more on Stephen Levine's insightful work see *Poiesis*, this quote can be found on p103

NOTE 9: There has been some discrepancy about whether these were indeed Einstein's words or as a result of a conversation Einstein had with someone else, if they indeed were not his exact words then it seems they were at least in line with what he was discussing during his conversation. The quote is cited p63 of *The Illusion of Separation*

NOTE 10: For more on Iain McGilchrist's insightful work see *The Master and His Emissary*, and for more on its relation to what we are discussing here see *The Illusion of Separation*, also it is worth watching this video of McGilchrist's work https://www.youtube.com/watch?v=UyyjU8fzEYU

NOTE 11: For more on mBIT see the book *mBraining* and also see http://www.mbraining.com/

NOTE 12: For more on Danah Zohar and Ian Marshall's work on SQ (or quantum intelligence) see their book *Spiritual Intelligence* or see http://sqi.co/ also it is worth exploring recent findings on 'collaborative intelligence' see https://en.wikipedia.org/wiki/Collaborative_intelligence

NOTE 13: For more on this 'field' and 'the unified quantum field theory' in particular relation with consciousness, see physicist John Hagelin's very clear and informative talk on the unified field of consciousness and our brain activity here http://www.scienceandnonduality.com/videos/john-hagelin-is-consciousness-the-unified-field/

NOTE 14: For John Cleese's talk on creativity see https://www.youtube.com/watch?v=Qby0ed4aVpo

MODULE FOUR: PERSONAL GNOSIS

NOTE 1: For more on the effects of stress on our resonance as leaders see *Resonant Leadership*

NOTE 2: For more on and how ancient Greek philosophy provides insight on our embodied, phenomenological experience of life see *The Illusion of Separation*

NOTE 3: For more insights from Peter Reason see *Spindrift* , this particular part comes from p182

NOTE 4: For more on recent studies and general information on heart-awareness, see *The Illusion of Separation*

NOTE 5: For more on Cynthia Bourgeault's insightful explorations into the wisdom of the heart, contemplative prayer and how these both form an essential part of Jesus's teachings see her book *The Wisdom Jesus,* the quote can be found on p36-37

NOTE 6: For more information on heart-awareness and heart entrainment exercises see The HeartMath Institute at https://www.heartmath.org/

NOTE 7: For more on somatic awareness please refer to *The Art of Somatic Coaching* by Richard Strozzi-Heckler and *Touching Enlightenment* by Reginald Ray

NOTE 8: This particular exercise was edited from p187-190 of Malcolm Parlett's book *Future Sense*

NOTE 9: This section about co-creative dance came from conversations with Alan Rayner author of *NatureScope* for more on Alan Rayner's profound work see http://www.inclusionality.org/

NOTE 10: For a more detailed exploration of 'whi' see Malcolm Parlett's book *Future Sense*

NOTE 11: For more on this see p261 of *Future Sense*

NOTE 12: For more on 'inter-being' refer to Note 4 of Module 3, and also see an exploration of the inter-relational Mind of Nature and World Soul in *The Illusion of Separation*

NOTE 13: A practical book worth reading is *Active Hope* by Joanna Macy and Chris Johnstone

MODULE FIVE: ORGANIZATIONAL GNOSIS

NOTE 1: For more on these three criteria of Peter Senge et al. see *The Necessary Revolution* p42-52

NOTE 2: For more on Sounds True see *Reinventing Organizations* or see http://www.soundstrue.com

NOTE 3: For more on this see *Reinventing Organizations* or visit www.reinventingorganizations.com

NOTE 4: See *Reinventing Organizations* as above

NOTE 5: This example came from p60 of *Adaptive Leadership*

NOTE 6: For more on Richard Sheridan read *Joy Inc.* and visit https://www.menloinnovations.com/joyinc/

NOTE 7: For more on FAVI as a case study see *Reinventing Organizations*

NOTE 8: For more on Zappos see Tony Hsieh's book *Delivering Happiness*

NOTE 9: For more on the ancient practice of Way of Council see http://www.heart-source.com/council/way_of_council_intentions.html

NOTE 10: Non-violent communication helps develop societal relationships based on a restorative and regenerative paradigm of mutual trust, respect and generative dialogue. An essential part of NVC is Transparent Communication which is where we speak in the first person, accepting responsibility for our feelings without accusing or projecting. This shifts our viewpoint from one of me-versus-you head-logic to a more connected transpersonal point of view. For more on NVC see Marshell Rosenberg's book *Non-violent Communication* and also The Centre for Non-violent Communication https://www.cnvc.org/ For more on using conflict as an opportunity, see p208-211 of Scilla Elworthy's *Pioneering the Possible*

NOTE 11: For more on Dialogue see p114-115 of *Flourishing Enterprise* and for more on David Bohm's original work on Dialogue see http://www.david-bohm.net/dialogue/dialogue_proposal.html

NOTE 12: For more on the Herman Miller case and dialogue in practice see p116-7 of *Flourishing Enterprise*

NOTE 13: There are a number of useful books by John Welwood, all very readable and insightful. The one referenced here is *Love and Awakening*, pxi

NOTE 14: For more tips on Stakeholder Dialogue Interviews see p245-247 *The Necessary Revolution*

NOTE 15: For more on this see p114-115 *Flourishing Enterprise*

NOTE 16: For more on Open Space Technology see http://openspaceworld.org/wp2/what-is/

NOTE 17: For more on similar collaboration brainstorms, see https://medium.com/p/3dec5b0e4651/edit

NOTE 18: For more on Swarm see http://swarm.gd/about-us/

NOTE 19: For more on the useful work of Henri Lipmanowicz and Keith McCandlers see the *Liberating Structures* website here http://www.liberatingstructures.com/

NOTE 20: Thornton's Budgens Heart-in-Business Limited was created to inspire and support companies in a new way of being, one that looks beyond just focusing on profit. *The dream of Heart in Business Limited is that companies care about our people and our planet, and take into account what we are leaving behind for our children and grandchildren.* For more on this visit http://heartinbusiness.org/

NOTE 21: For more on Arawana Hayashi's work see http://arawanahayashi.com/

NOTE 22: For a more detailed exploration of Social Presencing Theatre, see paper http://digitalcommons.wpi.edu/oa/vol5/iss1/9/ For more on Otto Scharmer's Theory U-journey and The Presencing Institute see https://www.presencing.com/theoryu

NOTE 23: The main source for this section on Appreciative Inquiry has been the draft report by David Cooperrider and Diana Whitney entitled *A Positive Revolution in Change: Appreciative Inquiry* see https://appreciativeinquiry.case.edu/uploads/whatisai.pdf Also see p 127 – 149 of Laszlo and Brown's *Flourishing Enterprise* for a detailed exploration of W-Holistic Appreciative Inquiry.

NOTE 24: Parker J Palmer's book *A Hidden Wholeness* has a wealth of practical information on Soul Circles, plus a CD to help practitioners. The quote is found on p184 of his book.

NOTE 25: Social Darwinism, as it is described here, is based on Herbert Spencer's nineteenth century perspectives which influenced the socio-economic logic of twentieth century capitalism and neo-liberalism, along with the more contemporary neo-Darwinism of Richard Dawkins and others, which perceives living systems and human agency as innately selfish. For more on how this differs from the insights of Gregory Bateson and recent trans-disciplinary findings see *The Illusion of Separation*.

NOTE 26: The main source for this section on Artful Organizations is the report published by Ashridge Business School by Dr Chris Seeley and Ellen Thornhill, entitled *Artful Organisation*, dated March 2014 see https://www.ashridge.org.uk/faculty-research/research/publications/artful-organisations/ Also additional information for this section came from Stephen Levine's *Poiesis*

NOTE 27: For more on Interplay see http://www.interplay.org/ for Applied Improvisation see http://www.appliedimprov.com/ for Sociodrama see http://www.psychodrama.org.uk/what_is_sociodrama.php for Action Methods see http://www.psychodrama.org.uk/what_are_action_methods.php for Constellations see http://www.systemicconstellations.com/

NOTE 28: For more on Daniel Ludevig's work see http://www.moveleadership.com/Home.html

NOTE 29: See p139 of Richard Barrett's *Evolutionary Coaching*

NOTE 30: I interviewed Fritjof Capra for an article posted with the global sustainable business network TriplePundit, which can be found along with other related articles on my personal blog www.thenatureofbusiness.org for more on Fritjof Capra's work see his latest book *The Systems View of Life* co-authored with Pier Luigi Luisi and also Fritjof's on-line The Capra Course http://www.capracourse.net/

MODULE SIX: LEADING ACROSS THE THRESHOLD

NOTE 1: The interim report for the Churchill 2015 21st Century Statesmanship Global Leaders Programme, by Nik Gowing and Chris Langdon, entitled *Thinking The Unthinkable A New Imperative For Leadership In The Digital Age*

NOTE 2: As above, p13

NOTE 3: For more on this see p186 *Conscious Capitalism*

NOTE 4: For more on Mac Macartney's exploration of authentic leadership see *Finding Earth Finding Soul*, this quote can be found on p126

NOTE 5: Scilla Elworthy's book *Pioneering the Possible* explores a variety of leaders, yet it is more than a book on leadership as it also contains great wisdom about how to live and lead in these challenging times.

NOTE 6: More on this and other insights on leadership as well as organizational and personal transformation can be found in Peter Senge's et al. book *Presence*, the section on the seven places of leadership can be found on p187 of the book.

NOTE 7: See p110 of *The Practice of Adaptive Leadership*

NOTE 8: For more on Gina Hayden's work at The Centre for Conscious Leadership see http://gcfcl.com/

NOTE 9: I interviewed Fritjof Capra for an article entitled *Embracing Systemic Thinking for our Firms of the Future*, see here http://www.triplepundit.com/2016/01/embracing-systemic-thinking-firms-future/ for more on Fritjof Capra's work see his latest book *The Systems View of Life* co-authored with Pier Luigi Luisi and also Fritjof's on-line The Capra Course http://www.capracourse.net/

NOTE 10: For more on millennials see the opinion paper co-authored by Anton Chernikov and Giles Hutchins entitled *Redefining The Nature of Business for the Millennial Age* http://www.exponentials.co.uk/#!opinion-paper/ctmx

NOTE 11: Of relevance here is the important work of Otto Scharmer, Peter Senge and others at The Presencing Institute and the MITx ULab on-line courses, see https://www.presencing.com/

NOTE 12: See p11 *Compassionate Leadership*

NOTE 13: As above p197

NOTE 14: For more on 'The Art of Hosting' see http://www.artofhosting.org/

NOTE 15: For more on Sue Blagburn's 'Adventures with Horses' see http://www.adventureswithhorses.co.uk/

NOTE 16: Phenomenology is a modern Western philosophy formed by many great minds such as Goethe, Husserl, Heidegger, Gadamer and Merleau-Ponty. It is a way of experiencing the world which transcends the objectification of Cartesian philosophy by understanding our perception as a co-participatory intimate conversation between our bodymind and world. We are in continual dialogue with our environment. Such a phenomenological understanding helps us move beyond the polarizing, objectifying, separating nature of our ego-lenses. For more on this see Chapter 10 of *The Illusion of Separation*

MODULE SEVEN: ALCHEMY

NOTE 1: Ann Baring's magus opus *The Dream of the Cosmos* is a wonderful soul expedition, this quote can be found on p362

NOTE 2: For more on the profound explorations of mythologist Joseph Campbell see both *The Hero's Journey* and *The Hero with a Thousand Faces*

NOTE 3: For more on Lao Tzu's wisdom see *Tao Te Ching*

NOTE 4: The hexagon is an ancient symbol and has been used in folk lore and esoteric traditions the world over. From a metaphysical perspective, this hexagon can be seen as a two-dimensional representation of a three-dimensional structure called a Star Tetrahedron, which consists of two interlacing tetrahedrons (pyramid shapes), a masculine one pointing upward and a feminine one pointing downward. For the ancient founding fathers of Western philosophy, such as Pythagoras and Plato, the Star Tetrahedron was understood to be a geometric vibrational logic permeating Life. Interestingly, recent findings from a pioneering quantum explorer, Nassim Haramein, suggest this pattern as being innate within the zero-point energy field (or quantum vacuum) that pervades our universe. For more on Nassim Haramein's work see http://resonance.is/explore/nassim-haramein/

NOTE 5: For more on this way of attending to reality see *The Illusion of Separation* p162

NOTE 6: See James Hillman's *The Soul's Code* for a detailed exploration into soul callings, this quote is found on p278-286

NOTE 7: If you would like to explore a more philosophical take on life as a love-journey see Sam Keen's *The Passionate Life*, this quote comes from p4

APPENDIX

NOTE 1: This Healthcheck was formed in collaboration with The Flourishing Initiative see http://www.theflourishinitiative.com/

SELECTED BIBLIOGRAPHY

ABRAHAM MASLOW, *Towards a Psychology of Being*, New York, Van Nostrand (1968)

ABRAHAM MASLOW, *Motivation and Personality*, New York, Harper & Row (1970)

ALAIN DE BOTTON, *Status Anxiety*, London, Hamish Hamilton (2004)

ANNE BARING, *The Dream of the Cosmos*, Dorset, Archive Publishing (2013)

ANTOINE DE SAINT-EXUPERY, *The Little Prince*, London, Egmont (2002)

BILL PFEIFFER, *Wild Earth Wild Soul*, Alresford, Moon Books (2013)

BONNIE GLASS-COFFIN & DON OSCAR MIRO-QUESADA, *Lessons in Courage*, Virginia, Rainbow Ridge (2013)

BRUCE LIPTON & STEVE BHAERMAN, *Spontaneous Evolution*, Hay House (2009)

C.S. LEWIS, *The Screwtape Letters*, New York, HarperCollins Publishers (1942)

CANDACE PERT, *Molecules of Emotion*, London, Simon and Schuster Ltd. (1998)

CARL JUNG, *The Undiscovered Self*, in *Collected Works of Carl Gustav Jung*, vol. 10, Princeton, Princeton University Press (1990)

CHARLES O HOLLIDAY ET AL, *Walking the Talk*, Sheffield, Greenleaf Publishing (2002)

CHGYAM TRUNGPA, *Shambhala*, Boston, Shambhala (2007)

CYNTHIA BOURGEAULT, *The Wisdom Jesus*, Boston, Shambhala (2008)

DANAH ZOHAR & IAN MARSHALL, *Spiritual Intelligence*, London, Bloomsbury (2000)

DAVID L DOTLICH ET AL, *Head Heart & Guts*, San Francisco, Jossey-Bass (2006)

DENNIS W BAKKE, *Joy At Work*, Seattle, PVG (2005)

DONALD SULL, *The Upside of Turbulence*, New York, Harper Business (2009)

E.F SCHUMACHER, *Small is Beautiful*, London, Penguin Group (1973)

ECKHART TOLLE, *A New Earth*, London, Penguin (2005)

ELIAS AMIDON, *The Open Path*, Boulder, Sentient Publications (2012)

FREDERIC LALOUZ, *Reinventing Organizations*, Brussels, Nelson Parker (2014)

FRITJOF CAPRA & PIER LUIGI LUISI, *The Systems View of Life*, Cambridge, Cambridge University Press (2014)

GERALD MAY, *The Awakened Heart*, New York, Harper Collins (1991)

GILES HUTCHINS, *The Nature of Business*, Totnes, Green Books (2012)

GILES HUTCHINS, *The Illusion of Separation*, Edinburgh, Floris Books (2014)

GRANT SOOSALU & MARVIN OKA, *mBraining*, mBIT International Pty Ltd (2012)

GREGORY BATESON, *Steps to an Ecology of Mind*, Chicago, The University of Chicago Press (2000)

GUNTER PAULI, *Upsizing: The Road To Zero Emissions*, Greenleaf Publishing (1998)

HENRY CORBIN, *Alone with the Alone*, Princeton, Princeton University Press (1969)

HRH THE PRINCE OF WALES ET AL, *Harmony*, Blue Door (2010)

IAIN MCGILCHRIST, *The Master and his Emissary*, London, Yale University Press (2010)

JAMES GUSTAVE SPETH, *The Bridge at the Edge of the World*, New Haven, Yale University Press (2008)

JEANNE C MEISTER & KARIE WILLYERD, *The 2020 Workplace*, New York, Harper Business (2010)

JEREMY RIFKIN, *The Zero Marginal Cost Society*, Basingstoke, Palgrave Macmillan (2014)

JOANNA MACY & CHRIS JOHNSTONE, *Active Hope*, Novato, New World Library (2012)

JOHN MACKEY & RAJ SISODIA, *Conscious Capitalism*, Boston, Harvard Business Review Press (2014)

JOHN SEDDON, *Freedom from Command & Control*, Buckingham, Vanguard Education (2003)

JOHN WELWOOD, *Love & Awakening*, New York, HarperPerennial (1996)

JOHN WELWOOD, *Journey of the Heart*, New York, HarperPerennial (1990)

JOSEPH CAMPBELL, *The Hero with a Thousand Faces*, Novato, New World Library (2008)

JOSEPH CAMPBELL, *The Hero's Journey*, Novato, New World Library (1990)

LANCE H GUNDERSON & C.S. HOLLING, *Panarchy*, Washington, Island Press (2002)

LAO TZU, *Tao Te Ching*, Translated by Stephen Mitchell, London, Frances Lincoln (1999)

LAYTH MATTHEWS, *The Four Noble Truths of Wealth*, Enlightened Economy Books (2014)

MALCOLM PARLETT, *Future Sense, Five Explorations of Whole Intelligence for a World That's Waking Up*, Beauchamp, Matador (2015)

MANLEY HOPKINSON, *Compassionate Leadership*, London, Piakus (2014)

MARSHALL B ROSENBERG, *Nonviolent Communication*, Encinitas, Puddle Dancer Press (2003)

MAX DE PREE, *Leadership Jazz*, New York, Dell Trade (1993)

MICHAEL BRAUNGART & WILLIAM MCDONOUGH, *Cradle to Cradle*, London, Vintage (2009)

NASSIM NICHOLAS TALEB, *Antifragile*, London, Penguin (2012)

NORMAN WOLFE, *The Living Organization*, Irvine, Quantum Leaders (2011)

OTTO SCHARMER & KATRIN KAUFER, *Leading From The Emerging Future*, San Francisco, Berret-Koehler Publishers (2013)

PAMELA MANG & BILL REED, *Designing from Place, a Regenerative Framework and Methodology*, Building Research & Information, 40:1 (2012)

PARKER J PALMER, *A Hidden Wholeness*, San Francisco, Jossey-Bass (2004)

PETER REASON, *Spindrift*, Bristol, Vala Publishing (2014)

PETER SENGE ET AL, *Presence*, Cambridge Massachusetts, SoL (2004)

PETER SENGE ET AL, *The Necessary Revolution*, New York, Doubleday (2008)

PETER SENGE, *The Fifth Discipline*, New York, Doubleday Currency (1993)

RAY ANDERSON & ROBIN WHITE, *Confessions of a Radical Industrialist*, New York, Random House Business Books (2009)

REGINALD A RAY, *Touching Enlightenment*, Boulder, Sounds True (2008)

RICARDO SEMLER, *Maverick!*, London, Arrow Books (1993)

RICHARD BARRETT, *The Metrics of Human Consciousness*, Lulu (2015)

RICHARD BARRETT, *Evolutionary Coaching*, Lulu (2014)

RICHARD BARRETT, *The Values-Driven Organization*, Abingdon, Routledge (2014)

RICHARD BARRETT, *The New Leadership Paradigm*, Barrett Values Centre (2010)

RICHARD BOYATZIS & ANNIE MCKEE BOSTON, *Resonant Leadership*, Harvard Business School Press (2005)

RICHARD BRANSON, *Screw Business As Usual*, Virgin Books (2011)

RICHARD SENNETT, *The Craftsman*, London, Penguin Books (2008)

RICHARD STROZZI-HECKLER, *The Art of Somatic Coaching*, Berkeley, North Atlantic Books (2014)

RICHARD TARNAS, *The Passion of the Western Mind*, London, Pimlico (2010)

ROBERT SARDELLO, *Silence, The Mystery of Wholeness*, Berkeley, North Atlantic Books (2006)

ROMAN KRZNARIC, *Empathy*, London, Random House (2014)

RONALD HEIFETZ ET AL, *The Practice of Adaptive Leadership*, Boston, Harvard Business Press (2009)

SAM KEEN, *The Passionate Life*, San Francisco, Harper & Row (1983)

SCILLA ELWORTHY, *Pioneering the Possible*, Berkeley, North Atlantic Books (2014)

SIGMUND FREUD, *The Future of An Illusion, In Civilization, Society and Religion*, London, Penguin (1991)

SIMON ROBINSON & MARIA MORAES ROBINSON, *Holonomics*, Edinburgh, Floris Books (2014)

STEPHEN LEVINE, *Poiesis*, London, Jessica Kingsley (1997)

STEVE HILTON, *More Human*, London, WH Allen (2015)

STEVE TAYLOR, *The Fall*, Winchester, O Books (2005)

TACHI KIUCHI & BILL SHIREMAN, *What we Learned in the Rainforest*, San Francisco, Berrett-Koehler (2002)

THOMAS KUHN, *The Structure of Scientific Revolutions*, Chicago, University of Chicago Press (1996)

TIM MACARTNEY, *Finding Earth Finding Soul*, Embercombe, Mona Press (2007)

TONY HSIEH, *Delivering Happiness*, New York, Business Plus (2010)

THOMAS BERRY, *The Sacred Universe*, New York, Columbia Press (2009)

WILLIAM BLAKE, *Complete Poetry and Prose*, edited by Geoffrey Keynes, London, Nonesuch Press, (1961)

ABOUT THE AUTHOR

GILES HUTCHINS IS A THOUGHT LEADER, SPEAKER AND ADVISER, applying twenty years business experience to his work at personal and organizational levels. Recently, Global Sustainability Director for Atos, and previously a management consultant with KPMG, he has helped transform a wide range of organizations (corporate, third sector, public sector and start-up). He co-founded BCI: Biomimicry for Creative Innovation, regularly guest lectures at leading Universities and Business Schools, speaks at conferences and expert roundtables, hosts transformation workshops and provides strategic consultancy. His previous books *The Nature of Business* and *The Illusion of Separation* have received much praise both sides of the Atlantic. Giles blogs at thenatureofbusiness.org.

To be a part of this future-fit exploration visit futurefitbook.com and join the Face Book community The Nature of Business

A SELECTION OF PRAISE FOR THE NATURE OF BUSINESS:

'*The Nature of Business is not just a very entertaining read, but also a redoubtable sparring partner. A must read for everyone involved in the business of the future…. and aren't we all?*'
Mick Bremans, Chairman, Ecover

'*A timely, paradigm-shifting book, reframing how business can thrive in the challenging times ahead whilst being a force for good…This is a brave book and a must read for those seeking to make positive change happen in business and beyond.*'
Hunter Lovins, President of Natural Capitalism Solutions and Co-Author of Natural Capitalism

'*Giles Hutchins has for many years been an innovative thinker based squarely in business and this book demonstrates that thought leadership; the book leaves me thinking much more clearly and feeling inspired to transform.*'
Paul Drukman, CEO of The International Integrated Reporting Council

'*Simply the best new book on business and management in many years!*'
Hazel Henderson, President of Ethical Markets Media and author of *Building A Win-Win World*

A SELECTION OF PRAISE FOR THE ILLUSION OF SEPARATION:

'*An amazing* tour de force, *the intellectual tour of our lives...Never before, that I know of, has the choice of life, true life, or the path of degradation been put before us with such clear equanimity.*'
Robert Sardello, PhD, author of *Love and the Soul: Creating a Future for Earth.*

'*Cutting through habitual denials and academic evasions, Giles Hutchins exposes the delusion at the root of our planetary crisis. And with a holographic richness of resources and disciplines, he discloses—indeed activates—the attitude that might just provoke our needed evolution. This is a wise and urgent text: may it be heard, and soon!*'
Catherine Keller, Professor of Constructive Theology, Drew University, author of *On the Mystery*

'*A treasure, brilliantly written...the best guide available today.*'
Chris Laszlo, PhD, author of *Flourishing Enterprise: The New Spirit of Business*

'*A wonderful book...well written, well researched and full of insight, this book will open your heart and mind to a deeper way of being in the world.*'
Stephan Harding, Head of Holistic Science, Schumacher College, author of *Animate Earth*

32866994R00181

Made in the USA
San Bernardino, CA
17 April 2016